Erikute,

linkėjimai iš Lietuvos!

Mamytė

2004-03-20

LITHUANIA

NATURE
TRADITIONS
CULTURE
CITIES

R. Paknio leidykla

LITHUANIA

EMBLEM

"Vytis", a white rider on a red background.
This galloping knight first became the emblem
of Grand Duke Algirdas in 1366;
the image is identified with the god Thunder.

FLAG

Three horizontal bands (from top to bottom): yellow, green,
and red, on a quadrangular cloth – the State flag as of 1918
(with the exception of the Soviet occupation years).

Geographical indicators

Territory – 65,300 km²
54% agricultural lands, 30% forest, 2% roads, 3% developed property, 4% waterlands, 7% other.
According to the National Geographic Institute of France, the geographical centre of Europe lies approximately 20 km north of Vilnius at 54°51′ north latitude, 25°19′ east longitude.
Lithuania's geometrical centre is situated 2 km north of Kėdainiai.
Borders total 1,846 km – 303 km with Russia, 724 km with Belorussia, 610 km with Latvia, 110 km with Poland, 99 km along the sea.
Lithuania occupied its largest territories during the rule of Grand Duke Vytautas in 1430: approx. 930,000 km²
Highest hills: Juozapinė (293.6 m), Kruopinė (293.4 m)
Longest rivers: Nemunas (937 km – 475 km in Lithuania), Neris (510 km – 234 km in Lithuania)
Largest lakes: Drūkšiai (4,479 ha), Dysnai (2,439 ha)
Deepest lake: Tauragnas (60.5 m)
Longest lake: Asveja (21.9 km), stretching through the Molėtai, Švenčionys, and Vilnius regions.

Climate

Transitional – maritime to continental
Average annual temp. +6°C
Average Jan. temp., seaside –3.6°C, Vilnius –4.7°C
Average July temp., seaside +17.4°C, Vilnius +18°C
Maximum high: 2nd 10 days in July, seaside – 1st 10 days in August
Maximum low: 1st 10 days in February
Temperatures begin to rise early in March, decrease at the end of August
Sunniest month: June – 9 hours of sun per day
An average of 1,642 hours of sun annually
Approx. 140 frost-free days annually
Predominantly western winds
Precipitation exceeds 600 mm annually
Up to 40 cm of snow in winter, more than 80 cm of below-ground frost

Population

Total population: 3,701,300
2,523,500 in urban areas
1,117,800 in rural areas
56.7 people per km²
Average life-span – 71.4 years
Women make up 52.8% of the population; greater proportion of men up to the age of 35–39, with a reversal among the older population.

Largest cities

Vilnius – 578,400
Kaunas – 414,200
Klaipėda – 202,500
Šiauliai – 146,800
Panevėžys – 133,700
Alytus – 77,300
Marijampolė – 52,000
There are 108 cities, 10 districts, 44 regions.

Ethnic composition

Lithuanians – 81.6%
Russians – 8.2%
Poles – 6.9%
Belorussians – 1.5%
Ukrainians – 1%
Jews – 0.1%
Others – 0.7%

Government institutions

A president is elected in the Republic of Lithuania for 5 years, Parliament for 4 years, and Municipal Councils for 3 years. Citizens of Lithuania over the age of 18 are eligible to vote. The Parliament, with 141 deputies, is the supreme legislative body.

Religious communities

Roman Catholic – 654
Old Believer – 57
Lutheran Evangelical – 54
Orthodox – 44
Reform Evangelical – 11
Eastern rite Catholic – 5
Muslim – 5
Judaic – 5
Karaime – 1

1 *St. John's (midsummer solstice) festivities at Kernavė*
2 *Symbol of Vilnius – the western tower of Gediminas Castle (14th–16th C.)*

Historical events

Ca. 10,000 BC – the first permanent inhabitants of the present-day territory of Lithuania settle in this area

Ca. 2,000 BC – formation of the Balts as a group

1009 – Lithuania is first mentioned in the Chronicles of Quedlinburg

1236 – army of the Teutonic Order is defeated by the Lithuanians at the Battle of Saulė near Šiauliai

1239–40 – unification of the State of Lithuania

1251 – Grand Duke Mindaugas is baptised

1253 07 06 – Mindaugas is crowned King; Lithuania becomes a monarchy

End of 13th–beg. of 14th C. – Lithuanians construct defence fortresses, many of which also become centres of economic life

Beg. of 14th C. – Lithuanian grand dukes begin marching towards Russian lands

1316–41 – Grand Duke Gediminas rules

1323 – Gediminas writes from the capital city to the Pope and to the cities of the Hanse, offering favourable conditions and inviting monks, merchants, and artisans to Vilnius. First written mention of Vilnius

1387 – Lithuania is baptized

1392–1430 – Grand Duke Vytautas rules

1385 – Pact of Krewo uniting the two huge states of Poland and Lithuania against the Teutonic Order

1410 – Teutonic Order defeated at the Battle of Grunwald

1422 – Mölln Peace Treaty, ending the wars against the Crusaders

1529 – passing of the 1st Lithuanian Statute, the legal act of the Grand Duchy of Lithuania – used as an example by neighbouring countries

1547 – first Lithuanian book – *Catechism* – compiled by Martynas Mažvydas

1569 – Union of Lublin, forming a Commonwealth of Two Peoples (Lithuania and Poland)

1579 – founding of the Vilnius University, one of the oldest in Central and Eastern Europe

1795 – third and final partition of the Commonwealth of Two Peoples; the greater portion of Lithuania becomes a Russian province

1831 – uprisings commence against the occupational government in the name of freedom and territory

1832 – czarist authorities close the University in retaliation against the struggle for freedom

1862 – the first railway and telegraph lines are laid in Lithuania

1863 – uprising against serfdom (abolished only in word in 1861) and against the Russian occupation

1864–1904 – banning of Lithuanian press

1883 – publication in East Prussia of *Aušra* ("Dawn"), a journal which made a great impact on the rebirth of the nation

1918 02 16 – signing of the Act of Independence

1920 12 19 – first professional theatre performance

1920 12 31 – premiere of Verdi's "La traviata" – first professional opera performance

1922 – introduction of the national currency, the litas

1924 – first national song festival

1939 08 23 – signing of the Molotov-Ribbentrop Pact, by which Germany and Russia divide spheres of influence in Europe

1940 06 15 – the Soviet army occupies Lithuania

1941 06 14 – first mass deportations to Siberia

1941–44 – German occupation

1944–90 – second Soviet occupation

1944–53 – armed underground partisan resistance movement

1988 06 03 – formation of Sąjūdis, a reform movement mobilizing the nation against the occupation

1990 03 11 – declaration of the Act of the Restoration of the State of Lithuania

1991 01 13 – Soviet tanks attack an unarmed crowd defending the television tower, and kill 14 people. The army occupies Lithuanian Radio and Television

1993 – first democratic Presidential elections

3 *Statue of Vytautas, Grand Duke of Lithuania, in the village of Perloja; erected on the 500th anniversary of the ruler's death (sculptor Petras Tarabilda, 1930)*

4 *Freedom Monument in the War Museum courtyard in Kaunas (sculptor Juozas Zikaras, 1925)*

Nature

Towards the end of March, groves of nut-trees start to blossom in the valleys of the Merkys, Šešupė, and Nevėžis rivers. It is the beginning of spring and within a week the earth awakens throughout Lithuania. Coltsfoot and violets unfold, orchard buds swell, bees come to life... One can hear the song of returning starlings, larks, and finches. With the retreating ice floes reappear the water dwellers – geese, ducks, and cranes. After a long (there is snow for two and a half months), dark (in December the sun only shines for 0.7 hours per day), and cold winter (the temperature has dropped to –43°C) – when everything living appears to have fallen asleep forever – one can really feel the return of the sun: all things, including man himself, revive. Lithuania is a land of contrasting climes. And what occurs in nature plays upon one's body,

5
Trakai landscape
6
Stork nest in Žemaitija

soul, and emotions. Long winters and dismal autumns bring on melancholia and introspection. With the re-emergence of the sun, man opens himself up to the world, and his thoughts brighten.

   Though the sea is right at hand, Lithuanians are a land loving nation – it seems that expansive waters made them fearful. Besides, the countryside here, with its hills, forest groves, river dales and lakes is pleasing to the eye. Back when the glaciers melted, immense torrents of water washed out broad and deep gulleys in one place, depositing gravel, sand, and clay in another. The gulleys became narrow, deep, steeply banked lakes: Tauragnas, Sartai, Asveja, Jūžintas, Gaustas. Chains of hillocks formed where the edges of melting glaciers sheltered; and among them small lakes, ravines, and marshes. This is the landscape of Dzūkija, Zarasai, Utena – Lithuania's most beautiful spots. The earth there is not fertile; where the soil is rich, in southwestern, Central Lithuania, the landscape is less exciting.

The mountains of Lithuania are in fact only hills. The very highest, Juozapinė, is not far from Vilnius and measures 293.6 metres. The tallest in Žemaitija (Samogitia) is Šatrija (227 m); from its summit one can look out over the farthest horizons. It is said that once upon a time giants walked these lands. Stopping to empty their sand filled clogs, they shook out one to make Girininkai Hill, and another, called Šatrija Hill. The majority of Lithuania's "mountains" are not famous for their height: Rambynas (near Tilsit), for example, is only 46 metres high, but was a sanctum for the ancient Lithuanians. This mountain abounds in legends, and festive national traditions were celebrated on the site even during the country's most difficult periods. They say that in

the olden times vestal virgins kindled fires on Birutė Hill (220 m) in Palanga. Birutė, a priestess who later became the wife of Grand Duke Kęstutis and mother of Vytautas the Great, also served the sacred fire.

There are unique hills in Lithuania known as fortress mounds. A hill situated in a place convenient for defence purposes, usually at the confluence of rivers, would become the site of a tribal settlement or fortress. The highest (142 m) and most important fortress mound is Gediminas Hill, which sits at the junction of the Neris and Vilnia rivers: from thence began the history of the city of Vilnius. Apuolė, the oldest fortress mound in Lithuania (noted in written sources as existing in the year 853), was the site of battles against the Vikings, and sits where the Luoba and Babrungas rivers meet. The largest, Bražuolė fortress mound, is located in the Trakai region; the square on its summit measures 2 hectares. Southern Lithuania has Rudamina fortress mound, visible from afar, for it was built on top of another high hill.

7
Fortress mounds at Kernavė – the site of a town of merchants and tradesmen in the 13th C.; the first capital of Lithuania
8
Stone museum in Mosėdis

9
Rambynas Hill on the right bank of the Nemunas River, close to the town of Tilsit (Sovetsk)
10
Aukštaitija National Park. View from Ladakalnis

11
Lake Kančioginas in the Sirvėta Regional Park
12
Žemaitija National Park. Lake Plateliai
13
Nemunas River Bend Regional Park. Curve in the Nemunas River from Punia Hill
14
Neris River below Vilnius

Four percent of Lithuanian territory is made up of internal waterlands. It is difficult to count the exact number of rivers. There are 758 which are longer than 10 km, 18 which flow for more than 100 km, and many thousands of smaller streams. Flowing out of springs, from lakes or marshes, they collect the rainwater, empty into the Nemunas, and thereby reach the Curonian Lagoon. The water of a great many of the streams, especially ones flowing through the forests, is pure and bordered by fresh greenery.

The total length of the Nemunas, the largest river in Lithuania, is nearly 1,000 km (it flows for 475 km through this country, the remainder through Belorussia). Between the towns of Punia and Birštonas is a site matched by few in the world, for here lie the great curves of this mighty river. A straight path northwards, from the beginning of the first curve and as far as Birštonas, where the

river once again starts to flow in the original direction, is nearly 10 km – by river the distance is more than 50 km. Winding back on itself southwards two times, the Nemunas makes a number of very complex bends. Nestled in one of these lie the Punia Forests, with every variety of tree known to Lithuania. Perhaps it was these bends which inspired Jan Długosz, a 15th C. Polish chronicler, to describe all of the country's rivers as being very sinuous: apparently after a day's travel down river, raftsmen could return across dry land to fetch burning coals from the previous night's campfire.

Lithuania, especially its eastern section, is a land of lakes: a band of them marks the edge of the glaciers which existed during the last Ice Age. Of these, 2,833 are larger than 0.5 hectares, and there are more than a thousand and a half smaller ones. All found in Eastern Lithuania, the largest are Drūkšiai (4,479 ha) and Dysnai (2,439 ha); the deepest is Tauragnas (60.5 m); the longest is Asveja, which extends for 21.9 km through the regions of Molėtai, Švenčionys, and Vilnius.

Approximately 28% of Lithuania – mostly in the south and in the east – is covered in woods. In the largest of them – Dainava, Labanoras, Gudai, and Rūdninkai – grow pine, fir, birch, alder, asp, ash, and oak. The forests are carpeted with moss, fern, wood sorrel, lily of the valley, violets, bilberries, blueberries, wild strawberries. Along the edges and in the meadows grow yellow Saint-John's-wort, white flowering camomile, grey absinthium, clouds of milfoil, and heaths of bent-grass. The woods yield approximately 150 varieties of edible mushrooms. Few Lithuanians would not recognize brown and redcapped boletus, birch-mushrooms, or chanterelles, and very few ardently dislike gathering them.

Up until the 20th C., approximately 6.5% of Lithuanian territory was taken over by marshlands; eventually more than half were drained. It is mostly lakeside or reserve marshes which remain. The largest, called Čepkeliai Bog (nearly 6,000 ha), extends through the middle of the Gudai Woods. One would have to travel 20 km to follow it lengthwise. The marsh appeared during the Ice Age: melting waters accumulated in the present slightly hollowed bog site until a

15
Dzūkija National Park. Water lilies in tiny Lake Zervynos
16
Cranberries growing in the Čepkeliai Bog
17
Black mullein sprout yellow flowers in dry and sunny meadows
18
Boletus – Lithuania's most valued forest mushroom

huge lake began to stretch out near the glacier. The River Ūla, carrying water from the lake into the River Merkys, gnawed itself a channel on the one side, and the Katra, a tributary of the Nemunas, broke its way out on the other. In time a marsh with a number of small lakes – Ešerinis and Ešerinukas, Dumblinis, Morė, Balnas – were all that was left of the former glacier lake. The marsh is a world of its own: in the middle, low lying ragged little pines with not enough cover to hide an elk, and marsh-tea and cotton-grass along the edges. At the approach to the bog lie mainland dunes once buffeted by wind, now covered with gaunt pine trees atop a grey carpet of lichen. Inside the bog are fields of cranberries, with great yields each autumn just waiting to be picked. Lithuania's largest bird, a type of grouse called the capercaillie, mates and nests in this reserve. Here one can also find blackcocks, grey cranes, and shrilling eagles. It is the perfect place for grass- and other kinds of snakes, and blindworms, and a spawning ground for viviparous, yellow bellied lizards bearing sphagnum coloured spotted stripes on their backs.

Another point of interest in the Gudai Woods are its hollow trees, a legacy of wild bee keeping. They can be found to this day in the forest and in the surrounding villages of Zervynos, Marcinkonys, and Margionys. The bee keeper used to cut off the top of a thick pine, cover the remaining stump, and with a

19
Endangered black storks nest in the remote areas of ancient forests
20
Pašiliai auroch reserve.
Wild oxen, once natural inhabitants of Lithuania's forests, have been re-acclimatized to this country
21
Tropical coloured kingfisher
22
White storks – Lithuania's national bird

sharp chisel-like instrument hew out an oblong cavity – a "dravė". He would fit the dravė with crossbars for the honeycomb. The equipped tree would become the bee keeper's property, and it was unheard of that anyone would extract honey from someone else's hive.

The ancient forests, once stretching over the entire land, were home to many different animals – wolf, bear, wild ox, lynx, deer, elk, badger, fox, marten, sable; near the water lived otter and beaver.

As the woods disappeared, so did the wildlife. There are no longer any sable, bear, wolverene, or flying squirrels, and elk can be found in only a few of the forests. Beaver ("bebrai") were nearly totally eradicated in the inter-war period, and had to be re-acclimatized. Proof of this animal's prevalence in the old days lies in the great number of beaver-like names given to place and waterland: Babrungas, Babrauka, Babriškės, Bebrinė, Bebrica, Bebrukas,

Bebrusai... In total there are now 67 varieties of mammals in Lithuania's woods, and approximately 50 species of fish in its rivers and lakes. The most frequently caught fish include perch, pike, roach, and bream; the most prized are trout and eel.

One can find approximately 300 types of birds in this country. Some of them winter, others nest in Lithuania; still others appear only in the spring as they return from warmer climes, or in the autumn as they fly down to winter in the south. There are circa 40 varieties of birds of prey – eagles, hawks, owls. Farmsteads come alive with darting swallows and twittering larks, the piping of starlings in the orchards, the song of the nightingale.

Historians relate the appearance in Lithuania of one of the most magnificent birds – the swan – with the name of Sigismund Augustus: the Grand Duke delivered this symbol of chivalrous love to his beloved Barbara Radziwiłł (Barbora Radvilaitė). Naturalists, however, claim that this bird finally settled here only in the 1930s. Their preferred spot is Lake Žuvintas, a reserve which is often called "swan lake" or "bird paradise". There have been 258 types of birds registered here, and many nesting swans.

Another place which appeals to birds is called Ventė Horn. Summer in Ventė Horn begins with the squalling of flocks of pewits, herons, curlews, and somewhat later – young starlings. Great throngs of birds gather here during August and September.

National Parks

Because of its distinctive and unspoiled nature, nearly 11% of Lithuanian countryside is protected territory. National parks, home to living ethnographic villages and an abundance of natural and cultural monuments, have been established in the loveliest areas. They are located in Lithuania's four ethnic regions: Aukštaitija (the Highlands), Dzūkija (the southeast), Žemaitija (Samogitia/the Lowlands), and Pamarys (the seacoast).

Of the 30,000 hectares occupied by the Aukštaitija National Park, 15% is waterland and 70% forest. Lakes, marshes, and streams bathe the old Ažvinčiai-Minčia Woods, made up mostly of pine trees, though one can also find fir, birch, alder, lynden, etc., and 4 entire hectares of juniper bushes at the edge of Lake Baluošas. The Park forests are home to a multitude of rare plants, berry fields, and approximately 200 species of medicinal herbs. It is no surprise that folk medicine remains popular in these parts.

23
Aukštaitija National Park
24
Dzūkija National Park. The banks of the Ūla River

The elk is the Park's largest inhabitant. There are also the predatory wolf and lynx, as well as squirrel, marten, badger, polecat, weasel, ermine...

Osprey, and their unusually timid and shrill offspring shelter in the Ažvinčiai Woods. Sea and imperial eagles stop here during the migratory season. Cranes nest in the remote marshy areas – their favourite is the Gervėčiai ("Crane") Marsh. Lakes provide the black kite with dead fish, and the boggy pine groves are home to the capercaillie, the most impressive bird in these parts.

Whitefish, cisco, apeled whitefish, and eel are the Park's most valued fish. There are also lake smelt. The Park has 139 large and small lakes; the largest is Lake Ūkojas (210 ha). On an island called Ilgasalė ("Long Island") in Lake Baluošas, sits a little lake which is 17 m deep, and connected to the larger lake by a tiny stream. There are also 2 small lakes called Bedugniai ("Bottomless").

25
Dzūkija National Park. Skroblus River water reserve
26
Čepkeliai Reserve. Ešerinukas – a small lake in the reserve
27
Dzūkija National Park. Merkys River from the Merkinė fortress mound

Ladakalnis (160 m) is a well-known site in the Aukštaitija Park. In pagan times, rites in honour of the goddess Lada, bestower of life, and ruler of heaven, earth, and fire, were performed on this hill. The loveliest view in Lithuania stretches out from atop Ladakalnis: from here one can see 6 lakes, fortress mounds, abundant forests...

Fortress and burial mounds, and a stone age defence line in Rėkučiai all document a very ancient past. Monuments with a more recent history include a church and belfry of rough-hewn pine logs erected by local craftsmen in Palūšė in the 18th C.; an estate granary, cemetery, and 6 watermills in Kaltanėnai; an exhibition of the 1863 uprising, located in the mill; and the old village graveyard, burial place of the rebels – in the village of Minčia. And nowhere else in Europe is there a museum of old bee keeping traditions as rich as the one found in Stripeikiai.

The ethnographic hamlets of Šuminai, Minčia, Strazdai, Vaišniūnai, Ginučiai, Stripeikiai and Varniškės form an unusual park exhibition. Varniškės II is an old hamlet of 4 farmsteads – barns with threshing floors, a smithy, bathhouse, animal sheds, stick fences, beehives, etc. – under the wardship of the Minčia Woods. Vaišniūnai sits on the banks of Lake Dringiai, at the mouth of the Švogena River: for 17 years, a demarcation line drawn up in 1922 divided the hamlet and separated the people both from their land and their cemetery.

Four fifths of the Dzūkija National Park territory (55,000 ha) is forest, and home to the ethnic Dzūkai tribe of people; they have been the longest to retain the old lifestyle, farming methods, festive traditions, distinctive buildings, furnishings, and manner of dress. It is all alive and being fostered in Zervynos, Margionys, Kapiniškės and other ethnographic villages, where the old trades and crafts of forest and farmstead, including bee keeping and grass gathering have not been forgotten. The Dzūkai are talented "god-carvers" and joiners, potters and smiths, fabric and straw weavers. If every nation were to have its "southerners" – a people with distinctive and unique mannerisms – then the Dzūkai would be considered Lithuania's southerners. They are a sincere and musical people with a lively imagination and a love of song and story-telling.

There are many cultural and historical monuments in the Dzūkija Park. A fortress mound with the tower of a partially erected fortress stands at Liškiava, on the banks of the River Nemunas (the fortress remained unfinished after the Lithuanians routed the Teutonic Order at the Battle of Grunwald in 1410). Beside it is Alkakalnis (Shrine Hill), with a mythological rock bearing the print of an ox hoof at the foot of the hill, and a 17th C. church and cloister nearby; the church and yard house 14 works of art.

The town of Merkinė is located at the confluence of the Merkys and Nemunas rivers. Vytautas the Great would rest here after hunting expeditions in the Dainava Woods. The house where Ladislaus Vasa, Grand Duke of Lithuania and King of Poland, died in 1648 is still standing here. The old part of the town, with its demarcation posts (Merkinė was granted autonomy in 1491), Eastern rite church (now a museum), 17th C. church (later reconstructed), and fortress mound, is considered an urbanistic monument.

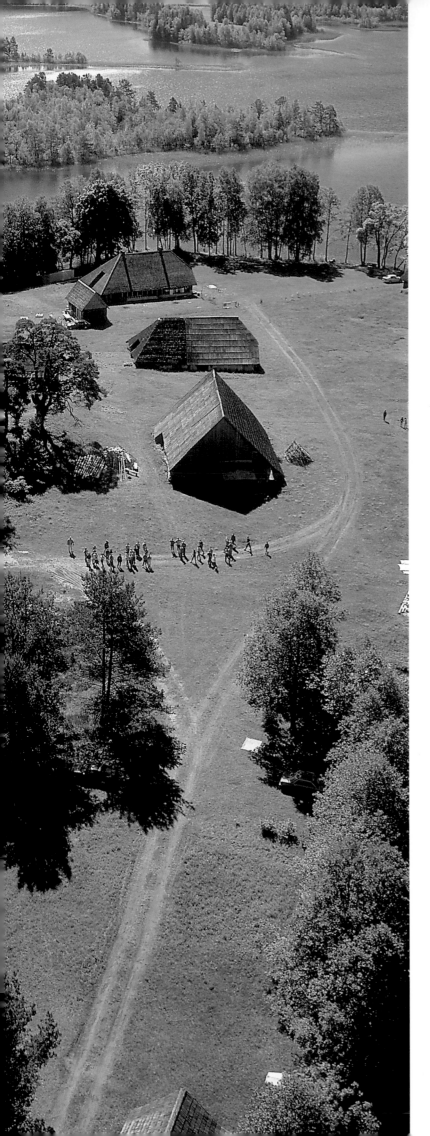

The River Nemunas flows through the western section of the Park; tributaries and offshoots of tributaries – a total of approximately 30 rivers and streams – course its entirety. The Nemunas, Merkys, Ūla, and Skroblus river valleys are exceptionally beautiful, and the Park itself extends to the Čepkeliai Bog reserve.

Sandy pine forests cover most of the Park. Here one can find nearly 300 types of mushrooms, and 45 species of moss. Steppe-like meadows stretch along the River Merkys. The Dainava Woods are refuge to perhaps half of the animals registered in Lithuania's Red Book. There is an abundance of birds, and one can even catch sight of sea eagles, osprey, eagle-owls and capercaillie. It is also the perfect environment for insects: approximately one

and a half thousand varieties of insects breed in the Čepkeliai Bog and surrounding woods.

The network of rivers in Žemaitija is two times more dense than anywhere else in Lithuania, with 65 streams flowing through the territory of the Žemaitija National Park alone. The largest, prettiest, and most famous lake in the Park is Plateliai (1,210 ha); it sits high up as if in a huge goblet, its shores winding around many peninsulas. Seventeen creeks flow into the lake, and only the Babrungas, the largest stream in the Park, flows out. Of the 7 islands found in the lake, Pilies ("Castle") is the most interesting. According to romanticist historians, descendants of the legendary Lithuanian Duke Palemonas once lived on this island; the walls of a stone cellar are remnants of a 15th C. castle. It is said that beggars returning from Indulgences in the parish of Žemaičių Kalvarija would wade across to Ubagų ("Beggars'") Island for the night, and that elk used to wander onto Briedžių ("Elk") Island to graze.

Forests take up half of the Park territory. Now they are mostly groves of slender firs, and not the impenetrable woods described by 19th C. romanticist historian Simonas Daukantas. One can still find marshes, watery meadows, unfarmed hills and sloping banks of streams, but the larger forests grow only beside Lake Plateliai. Here, especially in the Siberija Marsh, one also finds the greatest number of rare plants.

Today, the bear exists only on the Žemaitija coat of arms – there has been no sight of him in the woods for quite some time. The wolf is now the largest predatory animal here. The whitefish, a survivor from the Ice Age, is the celebrity of Lake Plateliai (it spawns naturally only in this particular lake). Plateliai is also home to the salmon-like cisco.

The Žemaitija Park has an abundance of historical and ethnographic monuments, including 6 cultural reserves. One of the most interesting is the urban reserve of Žemaičių Kalvarija. The Mecca of Lithuania, this village sits on hills near the Varduva and Pagardenis streams. Each July during Church Indulgences, the

28
Aukštaitija National Park. Old hamlet of Šuminai
29
Windmill in Žemaitija
30
A pole shrine from Aukštaitija at the Lithuanian Folk Museum

faithful sing hymns while making the rounds of the unique, 17th C. chapels which form the Stations of the Cross here. Two of the chapels stand on the Hill of St. John, from which one can view the expansive surrounding panorama.

A small 17th C. chapel and an 18th C. church, both built of axe-hewn logs, stand in the lovely Beržoras cemetery. The village's ethnographic farmsteads are roofed in wooden shingles and encircled with willow fences.

The town of Plateliai stands in the centre of the Park. Its environs (including the Siberija Marsh) shelter the remnants of defence installations and fortress mounds from various periods. Located near one of these fortress mounds are ancient burial grounds and a site for paying homage to the gods.

Kuršių Nerija (the Curonian Spit) is a peninsula of sand reminiscent of a sickle with its blade turned to the West, located between the Baltic Sea and the Curonian Lagoon. It stretches for approximately 100 km (nearly half belongs to Lithuania) from the

Semba Peninsula in the district of Kaliningrad as far as Klaipėda, where it is separated from the mainland by a strait measuring merely half a kilometre. At its narrowest, the Spit is only 380 m wide; at its widest – 3.8 km. Relative to the age of the planet, this is a recent creation – the Spit and Lagoon formed approximately 5,000 years ago. The sands continue unsettled even now: waves wear at the banks of the Spit (the area has diminished by 10 ha over the past 10 years), and the great dunes are flattening. There is a 9 km ribbon of wind-blown sand dunes between the villages of Juodkrantė and Pervalka, and another dune stretching beyond Nida to the south. Strong winds can raise the highest – Sklandytojų ("Gliders'") Dune (67 m) – by as much as 5 metres. The flora here are particular to dry sands, with exotic plant-life which does not grow on mainland Lithuania. This is not agricultural land; even fodder for animals is brought by boat from the other side of the Lagoon, from the delta flood plains of the River Nemunas. A thousand years ago, forests of oak, lynden, and pine flourished on the Curonian Spit, but a postal road connecting the castles of the Teutonic Order was built along its length. Settlements of people escaping serfdom and recruit levying in Courland and Lithuania formed beside this road. The pine timber on the Spit was excellent, and the ports of Königsberg and Klaipėda right at hand. The forests were both logged, and ravaged

31
Dzūkija National Park. Liškiava church and monastery
32
Aukštaitija National Park.
Apiculture Museum in the village of Stripeikiai
33
Nida. Lighthouse on Urbas Hill

by fires. The Spit slowly turned into a barrenness of wind-blown sand, and its first victim – the village of Senieji Kuncai – was buried in 1569; the inhabitants of Nida were forced to move to a new site 3 times. By the 19th C., a high and continuous ridge of dune had grown along the edge of the Lagoon, and the winds had buried 14 fishing villages, until finally, in 1825, father and son Kuvertas began to plant the dunes with trees. The present landscape of this region, dating from the turn of the 20th C., has to a great extent been created by man.

Approximately 15 million birds fly across the Spit during the spring and autumn migrations; some of the migratory birds even winter here. Great mergansers, northern geese, and swans flock in the ice-free bays of the Lagoon. The Lagoon's luminary, the burrowing goose, nests near Pervalka and Preila. The largest colony of herons in Lithuania has settled north of Juodkrantė: the tops of the pine trees shelter about 600 nests.

Come springtime, when the smelt begin their run from the sea into the Lagoon, fishermen from all over the country converge onto the ice. In the Lagoon, fishermen pull bream, varieties of pike and perch, rich tench and eel out of their nets. The flying "goatfish", which jumps over fishing nets, lives only in the Baltic Sea and the Curonian Lagoon.

There are a number of cultural monuments on the Spit. One can find pre-Christian wooden markers called "krikštai", which were erected at the foot of a grave, still standing in the small Nida cemetery. Markers for men were hewn out of planks from "masculine" trees – oak, ash, birch, maple – and were often shaped like

horses' heads. "Feminine" trees – asp, fir, lynden, pine – were used to make women's markers.

Juodkrantė and Nida still have traditional fishermen's houses: windows decorated with carvings, and small crossed wooden figures on the rooftops. A museum version of a fishermen's homestead has been put up on the site of a former village in Kopgalis.

Amber was harvested commercially at Juodkrantė from 1860 to 1899. The so-called Juodkrantė treasure – 434 pendants, beads, disks, amulets, and pieces of raw amber – was found here as well. A replica of these items is exhibited at the Amber Gallery in Nida.

In order to "protect Germany's northernmost port" (present-day Klaipėda), the Germans built a fortress in the Kopgalis Woods at the northern tip of the Spit in 1871. But with its strategic assignation forfeited in 1895, the fortress was abandoned. It was

34
Curonian Lagoon from Vinkis Dune
35
Thomas Mann's house in Nida
36
Curonian Spit. Still dunes along the edge of the Lagoon

restored in 1979 and opened as a Sea Museum with an aquarium and dolphinarium.

In the period between the two world wars, lovely summer homes were built in Juodkrantė, Nida, and Smiltynė; the Spit became a popular resort, and a visiting place for celebrated writers and artists. German artists in particular sought inspiration here; from the end of the 19th C. up to the Second World War, they came to stay and work at the Hermann Blode Hotel. This collective was known as the Nida Artists' Colony: their paintings, now found in Germany's great museums, depict the nature, the people, and the daily life of the fishermen in these areas. Scholar and geographer Wilhelm von Humboldt made Nida famous. He was especially fond of the nature here, and said that it "... is so distinctive that, like Italy or Spain, one must see it if one wishes to feed the soul marvellous sights." Nobel Prize winner, writer Thomas Mann spent the summers of 1930–32 here, and called Nida the most beautiful place in the world.

Architecture

The development of the architecture of a country, particularly in its early stages, has always been greatly influenced by local materials. Lithuania, like all of northern Europe, was a land of forests, and its native carpenters were therefore masters in the construction of wooden fortresses.

But not only wooden logs were used to build the fortresses of the 14th C.: they were also erected of brick and stone, utilizing a solution of lime which cemented with field boulders and produced a substance which has survived to this day. It was then that Lithuania inherited a tradition of Gothic architecture. On a broad scale, this important cultural development is identified with the name of Grand Duke Vytautas, for it was he who invited German artisans, experts in Gothic building, to construct his defence castles. The most original, largest and best restored monument to

Gothic defence architecture is the Island Castle in Trakai: the only water-bound castle in Lithuania, it was built on an island in Lake Galvė. Also during the time of Vytautas, majestic Gothic parish churches were either completed or started in Vilnius, Kaunas, Merkinė, and Veliuona; Franciscan monasteries were built in Vilnius and Kaunas, and the Benedictine monastery in Trakai. These were examples of early Gothic – massive constructions with high flat walls, pediments embellished with niches, and angular buttresses. Lithuanian late Gothic is characterized by its original façades and pediments with twin arches (the Thunder House in Kaunas) as well as wall decorations in geometric patternings of black brick. The greatest monument to Gothic architecture in Lithuania – a masterpiece of Gothic brickwork – is the ensemble of the St. Anne and Bernardine churches in Vilnius.

Features of Renaissance architecture can be seen in defence constructions and fortifications (the Vilnius defence wall at the Aušros/Medininkai Gates and the Bastille), in the buildings of the Lower Castle and the Church of St. Michael in Vilnius, the Church of St. Peter and St. Paul in Šiauliai, of St. Anne in Skaruliai, the Calvin churches in Rykantai and Kėdainiai, as well as in various other ecclesiastical and residential buildings. The intertwining of

37
Zapyškis church. 16th C.
38
Kaunas. Thunder House pediment. 16th C.
39
Skaruliai church. First half of the 17th C.

Italian Renaissance with Gothic and rustic architecture is an original aspect of the architecture in Lithuania.

Together with the other arts and sciences, architecture was a dependable tool in the hands of the Jesuits and other orders when it came to the rejuvenation of Catholicism. The flourishing of Baroque architecture in Lithuania was augmented by the religious fervour and thirst for honour of the local gentry, who did not begrudge funds for the endowment of majestic buildings. During the 17th C., invited Italian masters modelled the Baroque churches in Lithuania according to those found in Rome. The first Jesuit church – the Vilnius Church of St. Casimir – is a copy of the Il Gesù in Rome. The most esteemed monuments

to early Baroque in Lithuania include the Vilnius churches of St. Theresa, St. Ignatius, and All Saints. Grand gestures of the noble Pac benefactors left us the Camaldolite monastery and church in Pažaislis (near Kaunas), and the Church of St. Peter and St. Paul and the monastery of the Lateran Canons in Vilnius. The Chapel of St. Casimir in the Vilnius Cathedral is one of the most artistic Baroque mausoleums in all of Europe.

A Vilnius school of architecture emerged during the period of High Baroque in the 18th C. Its most eminent representative was architect Jonas Kristupas Glaubicas, who fundamentally reconstructed the churches of St. Catherine, the Missionaries, and St. John. Twin-towered Baroque churches were erected throughout the land, including in Jieznas, Kaunas (by the Jesuits), Tytuvėnai, and Stakliškės. Their graceful silhouettes became an important feature of the landscape in this Catholic country. Late Baroque forms were so popular in Lithuania that both Eastern rite churches, and Jewish synagogues took to

40
Panemunė Castle tower. 17th C.
41
Merkinė church. 15th–17th C.

copying them. They also made an impression on rustic architecture. Lithuanian wooden baroque is a totally unique phenomenon: folk artisans who built the churches and chapels in Antazavė, Lioliai, and Prienai adapted the canons of Italian Baroque to suit their own particular fashion.

The flourishing in Lithuania of the refined architecture of classicism is identified with the name of Laurynas Stuoka-Gucevičius, the architect who designed the Vilnius Town Hall and the Cathedral; he lived and worked in the second half of the 18th C. His buildings typify a Lithuanian interpretation of the classical

42
Aukštaitija National Park. Palūšė church. 18th C.
43
Fragment of the Smilgiai church altar. Latter half of the 18th C.
44
Lieplaukė church altar. 19th C.

style of Rome: they are perfectly and harmoniously placed in their surroundings, their ornamental features are distinct, proportions well developed, the use of antique details original.

Many of the estates of the nobility in Lithuania were also centres of economy, culture, and politics. They developed a distinctive lifestyle, and fostered the collection of kindred relics, of libraries and art works. Their owners sought to demonstrate their personal refinement and social standing on an architectural level as well. Baroque estates were especially ornate, the ensembles of magnificent buildings distributed in a free and open style. The later classical period brought a more symmetrical and rational composition, with the manor house strictly set apart from buildings designated for agricultural and other purposes.

Architecture during the second half of the 19th C. – beginning of the 20th C. (especially in Vilnius and Kaunas) was of a historical style, mostly emanating from imperial Russia and Warsaw. Typical for this period were buildings of rental flats, with imitations of the old styles (neo-baroque, neo-classical, neo-gothic, etc.), and an expanding aesthetic of eclecticism. There are many such buildings in the centre of Vilnius – for example in the areas around Gedimino Prospect and Basanavičiaus St.

In the 1920s–30s Europe adopted the ideas of the Bauhaus, and a rational style replaced the previous historical and modern architectural forms. Straightforward, economical, and simple architectural concepts reached Lithuania as well. Kaunas was the first to benefit from the work of Vytautas Landsbergis-Žemkalnis, a prominent representative of the constructivist trend. His designs, including for the Physical Culture, Municipal, Dairy Centre buildings, the Chamber of Commerce, Industry and Trade, and other structures were defined by a harmony of construction and stylistic expression. The War Museum of Vytautas the Great is a good example in the cultural sphere of an architectural balance of rational and classical traditions. The modern Sports Hall was designed by Anatolijus Rozenbliumas. One of the most majestic projects, though not completed before the War, was embodied in the huge Church of the Resurrection (designed for 3,000 people): in its design, architect Karolis Reisonas had incorporated the theme of the rebirth of the nation.

45
Komaras estate in the village of Raguvėlė. End of 18th– beg. of 19th C.
46
Kaunas. Interior of the Bank of Lithuania. 1928
47
Kaunas. Vytautas the Great Museum. 1930

Language

Lithuanians – approximately 3 million of them – speak a language from the Balt group of languages. Latvian is its only remaining neighbour language. Lithuanian has done well in preserving its ancient system of sounds, and a great many morphological distinctions; it has inherited a deep lexical stratum from its parent language.

A comparison of Sanskrit (ancient Indian) and Lithuanian sentences:

Dievas davė dantis, Dievas duos duonos. (Lith.)
Devas adat datas, Devas dasyati dhanas. (Skt.)
(God gave teeth, God will give bread.)

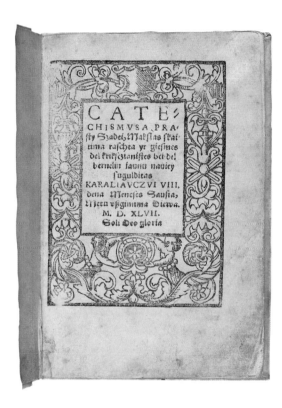

48
Pranciškus Smuglevičius Hall, early publications and manuscripts reading room at the Vilnius University Library
49
Title page from the first Lithuanian book "Catechismus" (1547) by Martynas Mažvydas

Lithuanian is an archaic language, slow to change: Russians, for example, must translate their 9th C. church texts, the English find Shakespeare's writings fairly difficult to read, but Lithuanians easily comprehend their own 16th C. written language.

Lithuanian is also a fairly complex language. Relationships among words are usually expressed via the forms of the words themselves (in English, for example, auxiliary words are used to this end). There are as many as 5 inflexible parts of speech: nouns have 7 cases; verbs have 2 aspects, 5 moods, 4 tenses, 3 persons, a singular and a plural, and in the vernacular – a dual. The language is rich in synonyms, riddles, sayings, and proverbs.

About a person who eats much and works little: works like a rooster, eats like a horse.

About a worthless thing or person: as useful as a billy-goat – no wool, no milk.

A woman's ingenuity: the "boba" could sharpen a knife on her skirt.

A riddle known by every Lithuanian pupil: when young I blossomed like a rose, when old I acquired eyes, and through them I crawled out (a poppy).

One of the most difficult trials facing the language was the banning of the press, which began with the suppression of the uprising of 1863 (the rebels fought against serfdom and the Russian occupation). Wanting to denationalize the Lithuanians, czarist authorities banned Lithuanian schools and the use of Latin lettering in the press – only Russian was to be used in schools, and only Cyrillic in book printing. (This tactic was later applied by

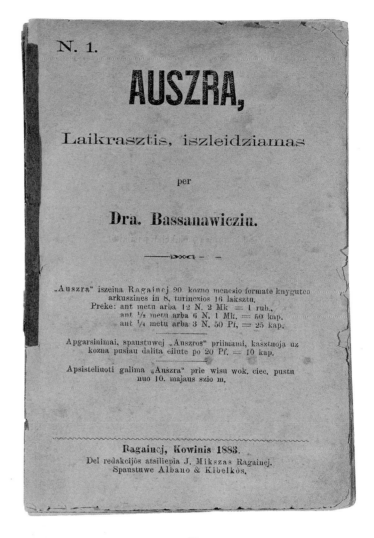

bolshevik Russia in Central Asia, when Uzbekistan, Kazachstan, Kirghizia, and Tadzhikistan were annexed by the USSR.) The ban was resolutely opposed in Lithuania: the years from 1864 to 1904 are known as the period of hidden, so-called "daraktorių" schools, and book carriers. Books and periodicals were printed abroad, mostly in East Prussia (which had a fairly large Lithuanian population) and brought into Lithuania as contraband.

There are various explanations for the origins of the country's name. In the end one comes back to words with common roots: *Lietuva* and *lieti* or *lietus* ("to pour" or "rain"). It is alleged that the name of the place might have come from the name of the stream now known as Lietauka, and back then as Lietava. The stream, the right tributary of the River Neris, flows not far from Kernavė – the territory where the State of Lithuania began to be formed. In time the environs acquired the name (only the suffix changed), and later the name was attached to the country. However, there is reason to allege in another direction as well: before the dawn of the creation of the State, the word "lietuva" meant ruler's army, later it became the name of the tribe, and later still – of the country.

50
Frescoes on the theme of Lithuanian mythology and traditions, in the vestibule of the Lithuanian Philology Centre at the Vilnius University. Artist Petras Repšys. 1976–1985
51
Petras Rimša. Lithuanian school during the press ban. 1939–1941
52
"Aušra", 1883 No. 1, – the first newspaper in Latin print of the Lithuanian national liberation movement, which was published from 1883 to 1886 in Ragnit and Tilsit (East Prussia), and allocated to Lithuania

National Holidays

Lithuania was not known for its Viking feats or its merchant voyages – it is a nation of cultivators, and its traditions come from the land. Everything surviving from ancient times radiates harmony and does not disturb the peace. That inner tranquility, harmonious interaction between nature and man, and profound insight into the existence of the world could only have come about when life was settled, peaceful, and consistent. A system of rituals assisted in creating such order in life.

The shortest days found the people trying to help the weakened sun through rituals celebrating the Return of the Sun; when they saw that it was in fact returning, they would celebrate the rebirth of time. Christianity identified the rebirth of time and of the sun with the birth of Christ – with Christmas; and so "Kūčios" (Christmas Eve – December 24) – is celebrated before the days become longer. The word "kučia" means a dish made of various grains, intended to feed the souls of the ancestors. Various magical deeds are performed, and fortunes are told on the day before Christmas. Once the evening star has risen, people sit down at the ritual table, laden with 12 (the number of months in the year) traditional foods. Besides the "kūčia", there is a porridge made of

53
Palm Sunday morning at Aušros Vartai in Vilnius
54
Decorated Easter eggs

barley ("grucė") which is followed by a drink of poppy seed milk, a jelly made of oats, doughy flat cakes made from scalded oats (later replaced by "prėskučiai" – unleavened biscuits), a pap drink made of cranberries, etc.

Fortunes are told after the evening meal. Lots are drawn by pulling straw from under the tablecloth: a long and straight stalk meant a good harvest of flax, and a long and happy life. Girls would listen to where the sound of barking dogs came from, for that was the direction bringing the matchmaker. They would count the number of logs they brought in, and the fence pickets they could embrace: an even number meant that they would soon marry.

Here, like in other Catholic countries, Christmas begins on December 25. Early in the morning, before the meal from "Kūčios" has been cleared away, one looks to find traces of visiting souls. The straw with its miraculous properties from under the tablecloth is fed to the animals. A pig is slaughtered before the holiday, and the Christmas meal must include meat dishes. In Žemaitija, a tureen of hodgepodge with a pig's tail sticking out, is placed on the banquet table.

A very old tradition, taken over by the Church, is alms collecting. At one time it began at Christmas and went on right to the Feast of the Three Kings (January 6).

Disguises – goats, oxen, horses, Death in the form of a scythe-bearing skeleton, devils – are important players in the rituals for the Return of the Sun. Costumed wanderers through the village bestow wishes for a good life, ask for gifts, and sometimes even run off with young women: it is thought that one stolen at Christmas and wed on "Joninės" (summer solstice) would make a good housewife.

The most important goal of rituals at the end of winter is to chase out the wicked winter spirits and to awaken the earth. Shrovetide is therefore a time of driving around the fields, visits with friends, sprinklings with water, and carting around and then burning a "Morė", "Kotrė", "Boba" or "Gavėnas" – effigies representing winter spirits. There must be a fight to the death between the winter spirit "Lašininis" ("Bacon") and the spring spirit "Kanapinis" ("Hemp"), with the latter naturally winning. Masqueraded wanderers – wild beasts, animals, beggars, gypsies – appear again; masks usually have crooked noses, sparse and protruding teeth, gaping or frenzied mouths. They are mostly carved out of wood and painted; beards, eyebrows and hair are made of leather, fur, fibre.

One must eat one's fill – 9 or even 12 times that day, so that "the belly would be as tight as a drum" – before the long Lenten fast, which lasts until Easter. Meat and pancakes are the most important Shrove Tuesday dishes.

Rituals for the Holy Week before "Velykos" (Easter) begin on Palm Sunday, with the blessing of the "verba" – little bundles of osier, goat-willow, and juniper branches. These plants give the earth vitality and fertility, and people health and good fortune. A living tradition throughout Lithuania is to whip each other with these to ensure good health and a clean body and spirit. The "verba" is then kept until the following year.

Holy Thursday is a day for tidying one's home – a guarantee that it will remain so all year long. An old tradition during Holy Week was to light bonfires and to run with burning sheaves of straw to ward off evil spirits. The Catholic Church as if extended the tradition of paying homage to fire by blessing it on Holy Saturday. In the ancient tradition, the old fire in the hearth was extinguished and replaced by a new one brought into the house.

Water was also blessed and sprinkled on farm buildings, food, animals, and fields.

Holy Week ended with Easter. According to a very old custom, it was celebrated for 4 days: the day of fire, of the god Thunder, of the cuckoo bird, and of ice. Decorated Easter eggs were the most important traditional food; a pig's head or a suckling pig decorated with greens, as well as cheese, butter, cakes, etc. were also provided. A plate of sprouted oats was placed among the dishes on the table.

The custom of decorating eggs to celebrate spring came long before Christianity. Traditionally, the bark of oak, hornbeam, or alder, onion peels, rye shoots, camomile, caraway etc. were used

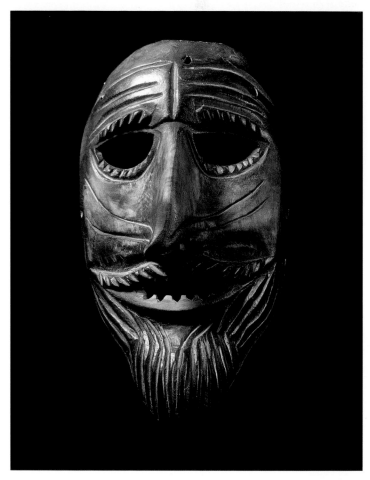

to colour the eggs. They were decorated not so much for their appearance as to give them symbolic and magical meaning. A gift of an Easter egg is intended as a wish of good health and all-round well-being. "Velykė" wanders around on Easter night and gives good children Easter eggs, and bunnies and roosters made of dough. Singers of Easter hymns would make their way around the village on the second day of Easter, wishing good health and harvest, and asking for gifts – especially Easter eggs. Breaking eggs to test the strongest, and rolling them, are played to this day.

The longest day (summer solstice) is accompanied by a celebration called "Joninės" or "Rasos" ("St. John's Feast" or "Dew Feast"). On that day, or on the previous evening, young women gather plants, especially medicinal herbs which miraculously cure ailments and bring good fortune. They weave garlands to decorate their homes and themselves, and in the evening, float them down the river bearing lit candles. In Christian times, wreaths were used to decorate wayside and farmstead crosses. People believed that the wreath was imbued with the eternal living power of plants, that it was a symbol of immortality, of the sun, and of the tie between the living and the dead.

In the evening – usually by a lake or a river, or on a little hill – all the people of the village gather around a bonfire; they sing and dance through the night, leap across the fire for strength and good health. At midnight, the fern blossoms. It's very difficult to pluck this blossom, for it only appears for an instant, and it is vigilantly protected by monsters. But great luck will come to the one who finds it...

From pre-ancestral times comes the belief that a soul ("vėlė") departing from the dead body is a threat to the living. Therefore attempts were made to protect oneself from vengeful souls, and to win them over to the side of the living. Like a great many other idol worshippers, Lithuanians arranged feasts for the souls, offered sacrifices, prayed, and performed rituals. The rituals –

55
Burning the "Morė" on the Shrovetide bonfire in Plateliai, Žemaitija
56
Shrovetide mask. Early 20th C.
57
Shrovetide games in Plateliai, Žemaitija

"Vėlinės" (Forefather's Eve) – usually took place at the end of November.

All of the "Vėlinės" rituals were performed in the cemeteries. People would come from around the district with food and drink, and feast for several days. At their own fireplace, each person would make offerings to the gods in order to strengthen the soul of the deceased. At night they would leave food and drink – mead – for the souls.

In some places in Lithuania, people would go straight from the church to the tavern, where a morsel from every dish would be thrown onto the floor, and drink poured under the table, in honour of their dead ones.

During "Vėlinės", graves are decorated with flowers and candles. The old traditions still survived in the first half of the 19th C., and were described by Adam Mickiewicz in a poem called "Dziady" (Forefather's Eve). As the poet said, his work was a word for word rendition of the hymns, incarnations, spells, and summoning of souls, etc. used by the people. The Church identified rituals of homage to the souls with the feast of All Saints (November 1).

Cuisine

What Lithuanian does not love tasty and filling food! Even work goes better after a hearty meal – and thus the saying: the scythe matches the dish.

Eating was once nearly akin to a ritual act. One behaved at table as one would at Church – eating quietly, meditatively, and with strict adherence to etiquette and custom. The head of the household sat at the head of the table, men on his right, women on his left. The mistress of the house sat facing her husband at the other end, with access to the food which she served. An honoured guest would be seated either in the master's place or beside him, while a beggar would be given the other end of the table. The head of the family first cut everyone a slice of bread. Putting a loaf of bread upside down on a table was considered defiling it; a slice or morsel of bread which fell to the floor had to be retrieved, kissed, and eaten.

Finding the family at table, a visitor would greet them with: "Bon appetit!" or "God fill you!". He would be fed not everyday dishes, but treated to "skilandis" (a special type of sausage), cheese, honey, home-made beer. In the spring, when fresh food was readily available once again, people would unexpectedly crack one another on the forehead with a spoon, and utter the words: "Fresh stuff!".

Festive and daily food was eaten according to the time of year. Animals would usually be slaughtered towards the autumn and in the winter, and more meat would therefore be consumed

58
Wedding feast table in a home from Aukštaitija.
Lithuanian Folk Museum

59
Cepelinai – a favourite Lithuanian traditional dish

during those seasons. Summer and spring would provide more milk, vegetables, berries, mushrooms, and grain and flour dishes. Black bread accompanied almost every meal; white bread was baked only for special occasions.

Porridge was the traditional food in Žemaitija. Lunch or an afternoon snack consisted of pancakes; dinner included soup – potato, cabbage, or beet – and meat; supper was a milky soup. Other daily foods: bread, smoked pork lard, fermented milk.

Favoured foods in central Lithuania included potatoes, boiled scones, dumplings, and soup.

The Aukštaičiai and Dzūkai liked pancakes with a sauce of crackling, cottage cheese, or sour cream, "grucė" (barley porridge), and soup.

Butter, cheese, and eggs were festive foods, as well as for the sick and the children.

Until the 16th C., Lithuania's nobility and gentry kept to the traditional foods, though their kitchen was never short of meat, dairy or other dishes. Later the wealthy classes began to use imported products – lemons, oysters, almonds, walnuts, wine, etc.

No dairy or meat dishes were consumed during periods of fasting, which were strictly adhered to for 4 weeks before Christmas, 7 weeks before Easter, and every Wednesday, Friday, and Saturday.

Traditional foods began to disappear in the first half of the 20th C., with the introduction of new dishes by professional culinary experts. Meat patties, "cepelinai" (large dumplings made of potato dough and minced meat), cabbage rolls, and vegetable salads became popular in the rural areas. The women learned to make various baked goods. On hot summer days, a favourite dish throughout Lithuania was (and still is) a cold beet soup made of fermenting milk, pickled or marinated beets, cucumbers, dill, and hard boiled eggs; it was usually eaten with hot potatoes. Along with bread, potatoes, which became popular in this country in the 18th C., remain the staple Lithuanian food. Boiled, they are eaten with a great many soups, and with hot meat and fish dishes; grated, they are transformed into pancakes, "kugelis" (pie), "vėdarai" (sausages), scones, and "cepelinai".

Beer gained popularity in Lithuania in the 11th C. It was brewed in central and northern areas – around Biržai and

Kėdainiai – as a requisite accompaniment for feast days, work parties, weddings, and ceremonies commemorating the dead. The head of the household or an invited brewer would produce a ferment made of barley (sometimes rye or wheat) malt, hops and water, with sugar added to make it stronger, or peas to give it more froth.

Home-made liquor, usually rye based, was more popular in the southern and eastern parts of the country. And according to historians, it was the Lithuanians who taught the Slavs not only how to pickle mushrooms, cucumbers, and cabbage, but how to make liquor as well. This industry continues to flourish despite decades of the strictest of bans.

The Old Religion

The Lithuanians had a rich archaic mythology and religion comparable to the religions of India, Greece, Rome, etc. Its most important feature was its close connection with nature: plants, animals, fire and water – the entire surrounding world was held sacred.

The Lithuanian Pantheon was similar to that of the other ancient countries of Europe, with gods for all states of life. "Dievas" was the lord of the sunny firmament, and the guard of order and harmony on earth and in heaven. "Perkūnas" was the god of thunder, and protector of soldiers and their commanders. "Velinas" (his name was later given to the devil, the evil spirit of Christianity – "velnias") was the guardian of animal husbandry, craftsmanship, and the dead. "Žemyna", "Žemėpatis", and other gods protected the earth, all that grows and breeds on it, and everyone who cultivates it. Not only the gods had control over the life of mankind – it was also in the hands of nearly all heavenly and earthly things, nearly all plants and animals, and natural phenomena.

Elk, oxen, boar, bear, etc. were connected with various beliefs. Of the insect species, special respect was given the dragon-fly, bee, ant, and lady-bird ("little cow of God"). Homage to the serpent was likely due to its odd appearance and startling glare. Serpents ruled the underworld, defended animals and the family, protected wealth, and symbolized the sun and the fruitfulness of the earth. People would keep and safeguard them in their homes.

A fire cult was important in ancient Lithuanian religion; it was

60
Small chapel at Kernavė. 18th C.
61
Sacrificial stone. Lithuanian Folk Museum
62
Iron cross from Žemaitija

Trees, especially ones with odd shapes, were identified as having miraculous powers. Once they adopted Christianity, the Lithuanians would hoist miniature chapels housing their saints into such trees. Even as Christians, the Lithuanians believed that the ash, willow, and juniper diverted misfortunes, warded off evil spirits, etc.

The World (Life, Sun) Tree grows in the centre of the Earth – that is its axis. Its branches support the heavens and cloak the earth, its roots reach its inner depths. On its top sit the birds, animals, sun, moon and stars. Under it shelter grass-snakes and serpents. Usually it is an oak tree growing on a high hill near a wide river in a large forest. Offerings are made to it, and it is entrusted with power. Lithuanians also honoured sacred groves where the sacred fires burned. The woods were home to spirits and deities.

Particular shaped rocks also had miraculous powers. It was believed that they embodied the spirits of the dead, and were therefore placed over graves. Food was left for the spirits of the forefathers and the deities in natural or man-made hollows in the rocks, which also served as altars for offerings.

based on the sacred fire of the hearth ("gabija"), and on open fires kindled in appropriate sites.

The fruitful land was treated with special respect. People would swear oaths in homage, kissing the earth before and after working on it. The earth loved only good people, it did not accept sinners. Transgressors would hear: "How does the sacred land bear you!", and "May the sacred earth not receive you!".

People also held water sacred and highly respected. It was forbidden to spit in it, or to dirty it, for in doing so, one spat in the face of God.

Burial Rites

The dead hold a place of honour in nearly every Lithuanian national holiday. In the words of poet Marcelijus Martinaitis, "Lithuania's most precious fossils are the bones of its forefathers".

Normally people would provide for their own interment garments: the men would hold onto their wedding shirts and the women their bridal veils. Deceased young bachelors would be dressed as if for their wedding, for it was believed that a person with no descendants would incarnate into a plant, animal, or infant, and bear an heir while taking on another form. Old people who had completed their work and left behind children, could simply disappear.

Hospitality was an important part of funeral rites. If there was no feasting, the deceased would seek vengeance. Beer, or mead, and bread had to be placed beside the dead person, and those attending the funeral were first given beer to drink.

Lamenting the dead is an ancient tradition; wailing helped the

dows and a door. Originally they were hollowed out of wood, and from the 18th C. nailed together from planks. Each family would decorate them according to their means, and along with food, include an axe, a flint, and a knife for men, a needle, a spindle, etc. for women. Relatives and people from around the district would gather to escort the deceased. If the coffin was transported by sled or cart, in the summer 4 small birch trees were placed in the cor-

63
Rasų Cemetery in Vilnius on All Saints' Day
64
"Krikštai", grave markers once used by Lithuanians from Klaipėda territory, in the Nida cemetery
65
Cemetery gates in the hamlet of Nirtaičiai

living to endure their loss and to maintain spiritual contact with the deceased. There was no exalted or hopeless tragedy – emotions were heartfelt and expressed with restraint, and the lament song occurred as a spontaneous and intimate improvisation.

For many centuries, Lithuanians, like their neighbours, maintained the custom of cremating their dead. The remains of Grand Duke Kęstutis, attired in splendid garments – including coat of mail, sword, lance, bow and full quiver – were laid on a bonfire together with an outfitted steed, hunting dogs, and falcons. With him went his hunting horn, and the claws of a lynx and a bear; on the day of reckoning his spirit could ascend the glass mountain to stand before the eyes of God. Funeral rites attended, his remains were cremated, and the ashes buried.

The dead who were not cremated were buried in coffins. In Lithuanian folklore, coffins are represented as having little win-

ners of the vehicle, and in the winter – 4 small firs. Hymns and ringing bells would accompany the dead body.

Lithuanian cemeteries are located on small hills: in songs, a hill represents a cemetery and paradise. The cemetery is surrounded by a fence and a gate – it is the "farmstead" of the deceased. The custom of fencing inand planting the gravesite with flowers is a very old one. Poles bearing small wooden statues of saints, miniature chapels, and crosses were once erected on the gravesites, but these days stone has mostly replaced the more vulnerable wooden monuments.

66
Distaff head. First half of the 20th C.

67
Earthenware jar braided in birch bark. Beg. of the 20th C.

68
Earthenware jug. Aukštaitija

Folk Culture

Due to the people's sedentary way of life, Lithuanian folk culture was founded first on archaic mythology, and later on Christianity. Religious feeling – their beliefs – underlay the way people behaved, their daily life, education, and culture.

In a wooded country, timber was naturally the material used for household items, work tools, and the construction of buildings. Hollowing was the oldest process used in the making of wooden troughs, tubs, mortars, buckets, platters, ladles, spoons, etc. Small boxes and various measuring containers were woven out of birch bark and lynden bast. The most ordinary work tools and household items – spoons, chairs, beds – were embellished with carvings; distaffs for holding bundles of flax or wool while spinning were decorated with the finest engravings in geometric, floral, and animal silhouettes.

Lithuania's ancient pottery traditions continue to this day. For centuries, clay has been used in the making of dishes for holding, carrying and preparing food, vases for flowers, and a variety of toys. Jugs and jars are decorated with birds, deer, geometric figures, etc. Vessels for bringing food out to the fields were made of two clay jars connected by a handle. Earthenware dishes were wrapped in woven birch bark to keep them from breaking.

A profusion of place names like "Rūda" ("Ore"), "Rūdiškiai", and "Kalviai" ("Smiths") indicates that there were many ironworks in this country. Local smiths provided the people with various work tools, weapons, etc. In time they

learned to forge ploughs and harrows, to bind wheels, and even repair various types of farm machinery. Craftsmen produced fine door locks, chest bindings, crosses, and candle holders.

The forge and bellows were a smithy's most important piece of equipment. Beside these stood a huge block and anvil, and a vessel of water for tempering the iron. The smithy was usually close to the road and some distance from the other dwellings; it was a place for the men of the village to gather.

Fabric for a variety of needs was woven at home by the women. Folk art researcher Paulius Galaunė identifies fabric with folk songs, claiming that they are both of a form embodying the spiritual life of the nation. Traditional fabrics were woven of flax and wool, the fibres coloured with plant dyes. The most decorative fabrics were bedspreads, saddlecloths, towels, aprons and sashes. Patterning was traditionally geometric and plant oriented, uncluttered, and with its own distinctive rhythm; its value lies not so much in technical perfection as in a very subtle combination of colour and design.

69
Ceremonial cloth. Aukštaitija. Mid-19th C.
70
Distaff head. Žemaitija. End of 19th C.

It is not known when linen first replaced furs in this country, but it is clear that in ca. the 10th C. women were wearing linen bodices fastened with brooches, long woolen skirts, and aprons embellished with brass ornaments. When it was cold they would don a thick woolen shawl fastened with a brooch or drawing-pin. The women were fond of jewellery: they wore several bracelets on each arm, rings on their fingers, brass or silver necklaces, and drawing-pins in their hair.

The clothing varied among the different regions. The most archaic were the traditional garments worn in Aukštaitija, which held onto the "nuometas" – a married woman's headdress – and the predominant white colour, the longest. The women's skirts were checked, sometimes striped, the bodices had short hems and were laced.

Clothing from Suvalkija – especially the women's colourful and highly patterned aprons – was the most elaborate. Headdresses included gold or silver galloons, and little caps;

they wore amber necklaces, and white linen shawls over their shoulders.

Women from Žemaitija wore a short homespun overcoat cut at the waistline, with finely pleated trim for buttons and buttonholes. Their scarves were multi-layered, their wraps white, checked, or coloured, with tasselled edges. Woolen striped wraps were worn in the cold.

Women from Klaipėda (Lithuania Minor) wore small lovely ornamented bags at their waist. Both women and men covered their heads with caps and hats; coronets of fabric and velvet ribbon decorated the heads of the young women.

Sashes of linen and wool homespun thread (later of factory made thread) were woven throughout Lithuania. Narrow or wide, they were designed for a variety of uses: to tie up bast shoes, to swaddle infants, hang bags and baskets, belt clothing, etc. Sashes were given as gifts on important occasions. For example, a bride would give sashes to all of her husband's relations, throw one over the gate, tie them onto roadside trees, place one by the well, the hearth, and on the stove in the bath-house. The patterns in sashes have very many archaic elements, magical and symbolic signs, and their own names: little steeds, roses, windows, oak trees, etc.

71
Women from Žemaitija in traditional garments
72
Gloves. Lithuania Minor. End of 19th C.
73
Sashes from Dzūkija and Suvalkija. 19th C.

German scholar Viktor Falkenhahn has said that the Egyptians are known for their pyramids, and the Lithuanians for their songs. There are approximately 400,000 folk songs in the archives at the Institute of Literature and Folklore; some songs have as many as 1,000 variations. Not so long ago, most village grandmothers, especially in Dzūkija, could sing dozens or even hundreds of songs. Many modern city people also like to sing: the tradition of folklore ensembles is alive and well, and folklore festivals still attract masses of people.

After the war, the Soviet occupiers took perfect advantage of the Lithuanians' affection for folklore. They even utilized songs to justify the occupation: experts in this field were directed to collect "revolutionary" songs, and were urged to create "collective" Soviet ones. Not only poets and composers, but the people themselves had to glorify Lithuania's "joyful" transformation as "a member of the family of brotherly nations". A State Ensemble for Folk Song and Dance, established in 1940, was the disperser of the new ideology: for 50 years it mutilated both a folklore tradition, and the consciousness of the Lithuanian people. Along with folk

songs, its repertoire included songs about Stalin, the bolshevik party, the "bright morrow of the kolkhoz". Its extensive and – it must be admitted – professional work led to its acclaim, and to an infectious spread of pseudo-folk kitsch. And yet, even during the period of the mass deportations, mandatory collectivisations, and resistance struggles, the real songs continued to be heard in the rural areas. Only land reclamation, which drove the people into settlements, and time (a new generation grew up in the 1960s, and with no room in the country, moved to the cities) destroyed a tradition which had survived for centuries. Later it was the town dwellers themselves who began to revive the rural folklore tradition: a broad folklore movement arose in response to the occupation, to the forced idea of the "merging of nations". Collecting folklore became a popular activity, as did learning songs and dances, and creating folklore ensembles.

It was predominantly women who fostered the traditions of singing, which is why there are so many terms of endearment, so many diminutive words, why the songs are gentle and lyrical, and why they reflect a woman's point of view. "Motulė" ("sweet mother"), "mergelė" ("maiden"), "artojėlis" ("dear cultivator"), "pjovėjėlis" ("dear reaper") – are well-nigh all the protagonists in the songs. Man is compared to a plant or an animal, and "white" is the most popular epithet, for it signifies beauty, goodness, and

worth ("mergelė baltoji lelijėlė" – "lily white maiden"; "bernelis baltasis dobilėlis" – "clover white lad"; "baltoji motinėlė" – "little white mother"; "baltoji aušrelė" – "white dawn"). The distinctiveness of the songs is also due to the intonation and the archaic melody of the language itself.

Songs are usually identified with certain acts or events, and are fairly strictly classified: work songs, calendar rites, family, wedding, children's songs, etc. Work songs help the people in their labours and enliven their moments of rest. Old war songs metaphorically represent the soldier's loneliness, his hard life, his longing for home: he speaks of bedding down on the mist and covering himself with the dew, with the moon for his father, and the sun for his mother.

Over the centuries (and sometimes following the example of neighbouring countries), Lithuanians developed their present-day folk music instruments. The very simplest wind instruments – whistles – came from sedge, a worm bored nut, acorn scoops, and the small bones of birds. Whistles are made in the springtime, when it is easy to peel the bark off the alder, osier, and

74
"Kanklės" – Lithuanian national instrument
75
World Lithuanian Song Festival

willow. Lithuanians can boast of having a unique wind instrument – "skudučiai" – a distant counterpart to Pan's flute. A reed-pipe which appeared more than 10,000 years ago, it is constructed of 5 (sometimes 18) little wooden pipes of varying lengths (8–20 cm).

"Ragai" ("horns") are Lithuanian instruments from before the time of our forefathers; they were used in war, for hunting, and for herding animals. Smaller horns were made of curved, or long goat horns. The horn would be boiled, smoothed, hollowed out, and bored to make holes; a bit of reed for blowing through would be forced into its end. Horns – bugles, trumpets, and "daudytės" measuring over 2 metres long – were also made of wood.

The drum, another instrument found in various countries around the world, was also known to Lithuanians from olden times. They would beat on drums during rituals to disperse evil spirits, and either to divert rainstorms, or the opposite – to call forth rain. The sound of the drum would summon the people of the village to a meeting, to church, to work, and to funerals.

"Kanklės" is a string instrument (with 3–25 strings) from pagan times; it was played when offerings were made to the gods, and during other rituals, including at weddings and funerals, and at the end of harvest. As a pagan instrument, it was banned by the Christians, and began to quickly disappear. It became popular once again as a national attribute at the end of the 19th C. – during the time of a national rebirth.

76
St. Francis. Žemaitija
77
St. George. Žemaitija. End of 19th C.
78
Vincas Svirskis. The Last Supper. Detail of a cross
79
Pole shrine with St. Florian in Plateliai, Žemaitija

Though fostering pagan traditions even in Christian times, Lithuania began to gain fame as a land of crosses. Crosses and miniature chapels with statues of the saints stood at the roadsides, and in farmsteads and cemeteries. The people called the saints "dievukai" ("little gods"). With their homespun coats, bast shoes, scarves, etc. the small statues were reminiscent more of villagers than of canonized saints. Favourites included statues of those saints who had certain duties and powers to safeguard the people and their livestock from illness and thieves, and to protect the home from fire. Very often one found the "Rūpintojėlis" – a woeful Christ figure, meditative and full of worries – head propped on hand, resting in the miniature chapel. People were fond of

images of the Mother of God, Christ on the Cross, St. Isidore – protector of farmers, St. George – protector of animals, and St. Florian – defender against fire.

Along with book carriers, "god-makers" were the careful tenders of a distinctive feature of the national culture. For a piece of bread or clothing, these eccentrics would hew out a statue of a patron saint for the owner of a farmstead. The majority of god-makers remain anonymous to this day. One of the few to have made it into the annals of history is Vincas Svirskis, who lived and worked in central Lithuania; during his lifetime, he hewed more than 200 original "pole chapels" and crosses out of oak.

During the Soviet occupation, attempts were made to suppress cross making along with most other Lithuanian traditions. A great many of the old pole chapels and crosses were demolished, and severe punishment threatened those who built new ones. Soviet bulldozers frequently ravaged the Hill of Crosses near Šiauliai – a site where, on various occasions for more than 100 years, people

had been erecting crosses. The morning after such "cleansings", however, the hill would always be adorned with new crosses. At the same time, the occupational forces pretended to foster the tradition of wood sculpting: the Witches' Hill in Juodkrantė, Čiurlionis Road near Druskininkai, and Ablinga village in Žemaitija were all decorated with memorial sculptures.

Of the old household items, trousseau chests filled with fabrics and special clothing were particularly artistic. Like crosses, statues of saints, and engravings, wooden chests had their own travelling craftsmen who specialized in this work. Each artisan decorated them in his own way – with stylized flowers, birds, or stars. The colour green was combined with yellow, white with red, yellow and white with blue... They were bright, but beautifully harmonized, and the drawing itself carefully executed and rhythmic. Not only chests, but other wooden things – spoon holders, cupboards, dressers, and shutters – were also decorated in this way.

80
Aukštaitija farmstead. Lithuanian Folk Museum
81
The Eighth Station of the Cross
82
Wooden chest. Lithuania Minor. Latter half of the 19th C.
83
Wooden chest. Aukštaitija. Latter half of the 19th C.

Paintings displayed in the churches during solemn rites and on holy days, especially ones famed for being miraculous, were a source of inspiration for the people. Pictures of the saints, painted on boards by rural artists, were installed in miniature chapels. Hanging in the most honoured place in every home, on the wall just below the ceiling and usually facing the entrance, were images painted on canvas or printed on paper of the home patrons and guardians – Christ on the Cross, Sorrowing Mother of God, St. George, St. Anthony. Religious subjects were understood, depicted, and composed in their own way. Their psychological state was represented in a manner accessible to all: sorrow was portrayed very simply, with huge tears running down the face of a grieving Mother of God... Quite a number of talented primitive folk artists – Monika Bičiūnienė, Sofija Katkevičienė, and others – depicting images of daily life, landscapes, and portraits have emerged in our time.

84
Pieta. End of 19th C.
85
St. Joseph and other saints. End of 19th C.
86
St. Barbara. 19th C.
87
The Crucifixion. 1772

61

Professional Culture

The diversity in Lithuanian culture was formed by the multi-ethnic legacy of the Grand Duchy of Lithuania (GDL), a national culture which re-awakened at the end of the 19th C., one which revived as a result of various exchanges in the inter-war period, and the influence of the modern culture of Europe.

The first professional artists in this country were foreigners; painters of Lithuanian descent – romantics and idealists – began to manifest only during the second half of the 18th C. The Vilnius school of art (1793–1832), which unified artistic life, fostered the arts, and developed a sense of the aesthetic (with features of romanticism, classicism, and realism), was of special significance to the development of art at that time. Artistic life diminished in the later 1800s: during the rule of the Russian czars, higher art schools were closed in Lithuania, and artists travelled abroad to study. With a change in the political situation in the 20th C., they returned with new aesthetic ideas to an increasingly more liberal Vilnius. The first art exhibition took place in 1907: along with folk art, it presented the work of 23 professional artists. The exhibition had far-reaching acclaim, consolidated the dispersed artists, and provided impetus for further development. Its historical significance also lies in the fact that Lithuania's most famous artist, painter and composer Mikalojus Konstantinas Čiurlionis (1875–1911) presented his works here to the Lithuanian intelligentsia for the first time. One could say that not only were his paintings visibly different from other works at the first exhibitions, but that they have never been surpassed by any other Lithuanian. The creativity of this artist (with his original and fantastic view of the world), who imparted imagery and sought for the likeness of painting in his music, and who transmitted the essence of musical structure into his painting, was fed both by the intellectual atmosphere of the beginning of the 20th C., and by the rise of a national art form.

Cultural life during the inter-war period rallied in Kaunas. New national art institutions and artists' associations were formed there. The Kaunas Art School, with the most prominent artists of the time as teachers, was established in 1922. The school administration would send both perspective instructors, and talented students abroad to train and to study.

Forward leaps in technology, unrestricted borders, and a continuously quickening tempo of life formulated *art deco,* a modern international style conforming to the most important postulates of mass culture. Modern office buildings, and homes for the new functionaries and intelligentsia in Kaunas required furniture, household items, and art works. Such things were usually imported from abroad, but their contemporary form had a huge effect first on the local style of advertising, and later on many other spheres of life. During the inter-war period, *art deco* brought a real revolution to Lithuania and its predominantly agrarian lifestyle. Even Juozas Zikaras, a sculptor with moderate views, took to portraying a modern Madonna: in his bas-relief, a short-haired woman wearing a finely-pleated dress and high-heeled shoes holds an infant who is playing with her long necklace. *Art deco* was also easily popularized because its principles corresponded to a so-called "national style".

In 1932, a society of artists was founded under the name "Ars"; they declared themselves creators of both modern and national art. Its members based their work on the traditions of folk art, especially sculpture. Fully cognizant of the Parisian art scene, they identified that tradition with modernity. The most famous artists of the time belonged to "Ars", so it is understandable that they made a serious impact on Lithuanian art culture. The art of the inter-war period, modernized and searching for a national identity, laid the path for the art of the second half of the 20th C.

The Second World War, and the 50 years of occupation which followed, severed the logical development of art in Lithuania. Art works from the inter-war period were proclaimed nationalistic, formalistic, bourgeois. Art was meant to serve politics. And post-war social realist art was in fact primitive propaganda. Optimistic images of work, Party figures, portraits of war and

88
M.K. Čiurlionis. Springtime (section).
1907–1908
89
Juozas Mikėnas. First Swallows. 1964

90
Viktoras Vizgirda. Village street with miniature chapel. 1939
91
Antanas Samuolis. White apple-tree. 1931–1932
92
Šarūnas Sauka. Thaw. 1991

work heroes (milk-maids in particular), and model life scenes were intended to create a joyful backdrop to the bloody period of partisan struggles.

After 1956, and the initiation of a "thaw" in the Soviet Union, certain modern forms of expression began to be tolerated. There could, however, be no change in ideology, and barely 10 years later, the so-called freedoms came to an end. But though official art was strictly censored, there were non-official exhibitions. The innovative and non-conformist works of "the silent modernists" were presented in the homes of artists, creative association venues, "Vaga" publishing house, and elsewhere. As in the inter-war period, confrontation with an inimical ideology led to the fostering of a national identity. Artists reverted to folk art, history, folklore, and officially prohibited Christianity. Many decades of compromise and conflict prompted introspection and pessimism: painter Šarūnas Sauka is the most striking example of that particular spiritual structure.

93
Mindaugas Navakas. Shield. 1980.
M. Mažvydas Sculpture Park in Klaipėda
94
Adri A.C. de Fluiter. Small Monument for Humanity. 1995.
Park of Europe

Slav (Russianized) and Latin languages were used in both church and secular affairs in the multi-ethnic GDL. However, adherents of a spreading Protestantism endeavoured to develop their ideas in the national tongue; thus the appearance of the first Lithuanian book – a Catechism – in Königsberg, neighbouring East Prussia, in 1547. It was compiled by Martynas Mažvydas, who also wrote a suggestive introduction in verse; he is thus known as the founder of Lithuanian literature. But two centuries later, Lithuanian writing was still only of a religious nature. Kristijonas Donelaitis, founder of Lithuanian secular literature, and author of the epic poem *The Seasons*, lived and wrote in the 18th C. One of Lithuania's most distinctive historical literary figures was Maironis (1862–1932), who wrote poetry and encouraged a national consciousness. Towards the end of the last century, his poetry – transformed into folk songs – rang out as the hymns of the "singing revolution". But otherwise, a traditional concept of nationalism, wherein language is considered the most important harbinger, is too narrow to describe some of the people who contributed to Lithuanian writing. Nineteenth-century poet Adam Mickiewicz was formed by the cultural tradition of the

ADOMAS MICKEVIČIUS

GDL: his native tongue was Polish, but he identified himself with Lithuania, its culture, and its history. Twentieth century poet Oscar Miłosz, born on territory which once belonged to Lithuania, wrote in French, but considered himself a Lithuanian, and spent the major part of his life in the role of Lithuanian consul in France. His relation, writer and Nobel Prize laureate Czesław Miłosz, carries on that same cultural tradition: born and raised in central Lithuania, a graduate of the Vilnius University, he writes in Polish – but even in his Nobel Prize acceptance speech, he raised issues pertaining to Lithuania.

The inter-war period provided highly favourable conditions for the advancement of literature: writers were encouraged by government institutions and publishing houses, by a progressive level of culture, and by an interest in literature within the society (45 novels were published in 1935–6 alone). Realistic narrative literature had tremendous vitality and portrayed the spiritual beauty and psychological depth of the rural people. Western trends in art reached Lithuania. Symbolism apparently most approximated the Lithuanian mentality, for it became the predominant poetic aesthetic, thereby enriching prosody, and expanding metaphorism.

Those who sought to sovietize Lithuania skilfully took advantage of the great authority of its writers: in 1940 the marching songs of the Red Army as it occupied the country were based on the passionate Soviet verse written by pure lyricist Salomėja

95
Gediminas Jokubonis.
Adam Mickiewicz Memorial in Vilnius. 1980

96-97
Rimtautas Gibavičius.
Historical portraits – Simonas Daukantas
and Antanas Baranauskas. 1989.
Sgraffiti in the Philology Faculty at Vilnius University

Nėris, laureate of the State Prize in 1936. The new "values" were also propagated by talented prose and journalistic writer Petras Cvirka.

The atmosphere of uncertainty and fear after the war formulated a people existing with a survival instinct. At a writers' congress in 1946, a novel by Balys Sruoga entitled *Forest of the Gods,* a sarcastic account of personal experiences in the Stutthof concentration camp, was called "a cynical mockery of the victims of German invaders", and the lyric poetry of Eduardas Mieželaitis (laureate of the Lenin Prize in 1962) – "an abomination". Dismissal from the Union of Writers, and accompanying complications, even repressions, were a very real threat to anyone guilty of the least insubordination. Balys Sruoga, Vincas Mykolaitis-Putinas, Jonas Graičiūnas and other writers were forced to deplore their "mistakes" and to promise to "vindicate the name of the Soviet writer". People chose their own fate. After being summoned to the NKVD in 1945 (which meant either recruitment or arrest), poet Bronius Krivickas joined the ranks of the partisans. Another poet, Kostas Kubilinskas, came on his own and offered his services – for "one had to survive". The former was betrayed, and killed in 1952; the latter found the right moment, and shot poet and partisan Benediktas Labėnas dead in his sleep – for that he was given the right to live and to continue writing.

Some time later, psychiatric hospitals became a tool even more effective than NKVD prison cells: in the days when the writings of

Lenin publicly replaced the Bible, opposition surely symbolized insanity. Not only repression motivated adaptability; there was also a system of titles and prizes, and quite a few members of the Union of Writers were able to devote themselves entirely to their creative work, and thus to survive fairly well.

1965 – when Vytautas Žalakevičius directed *No-one wanted to die*, a well-known film about the post-war period – was a turning point for Lithuanian film and literature. The terror generation was replaced by the thaw generation – without the oppression of the past, its self-respect recovered. The poetry of that time, though frequently compromised, was well-versed in the language of symbol and metaphor, and it carefully tended the aspirations of freedom for the nation. Volumes of poetry by Justinas Marcinkevičius, Algimantas Baltakis, Sigitas Geda, Judita Vaičiūnaitė, and Marcelijus Martinaitis were published in editions of ca. twenty thousand – astounding in such a small country! – and were bought up immediately.

When the Iron Curtain lifted, the works of Lithuanian emigrés Marius Katiliškis, Bernardas Brazdžionis, Alfonsas Nyka-Niliūnas, Eduardas Cinzas, Tomas Venclova – once familiar to only a handful of the enlightened – became the assets of the nation.

Unequalled opportunities emerged for the dispersion of Lithuanian culture abroad. The world discovered Lithuanian poetry, music (the works of com-

98
Petras Repšys. Little cowherd. 1978
99
Stanislovas Kuzma. Festival of Muses.
Sculpture above the entrance to the National Drama Theatre. 1981

posers Osvaldas Balakauskas, Bronius Kutavičius, Algirdas Martinaitis), and art (Dalia Kasčiūnaitė, Stasys Eidrigevičius, Šarūnas Sauka). Lithuanian musicians – the Chamber Orchestra under Saulius Sondeckis, the Vilnius and the Čiurlionis Quartets – were already well known abroad even during the occupation years; in the past years, the careers of singers Violeta Urmanavičiūtė-Urmana and Sergejus Larinas, violinist Vilhelmas Čepinskis, and others, have blossomed successfully on stages around the world.

Lithuanian theatre became widely celebrated thanks to director Eimuntas Nekrošius, who has won the highest European theatre awards. His productions of *Hamlet, Macbeth* and *Othello* are shown to great acclaim on international stages.

The works of photographers Algimantas Sutkus, Romualdas Rakauskas, Aleksandras Macijauskas, Vitas Luckus, Stanislovas Žvirgždas and others have earned Lithuania the reputation of being a nation of photographers. Directors Vytautas Žalakevičius, Šarūnas Bartas, Audrius Stonys, and actors Donatas Banionis and Juozas Budraitis have brought fame to Lithuanian film; Eglė Špokaitė has exalted Lithuanian ballet.

The institutional core of Lithuania's cultural life includes 12 theatres, 84 museums, 1,500 libraries, 3 symphony orchestras, and the national philharmonic. Traditional song festivals take place every 5 years. There are a great many international festivals: academic music – the Vilnius Summer Festival, St. Christoph, Trakai, "Banchetto musicale", quartets, etc.; folklore – "Skamba, skamba kankliai" and "Baltica"; jazz festivals in Kaunas, Vilnius, and Birštonas; film – "Kino pavasaris"; poetry – "Poezijos pavasaris"; the Thomas Mann Festival in Nida; city festivals in Vilnius, Kaunas, Klaipėda, etc.

Vilnius

A city with a northern-like reserve, laid out around a principal axis – the River Neris – and rhythmically rising to the outlying hills. Surrounded on all sides by forests which approach the city centre along the river banks and on the hillsides. A valley at the confluence of the Neris and Vilnia rivers, its terraces, and hills are a landscape formed not only by glaciers, but by waters of the rivers, springs, and rain. No other city on the plains of Eastern Europe has such surroundings – and man need not bother trying to compete with the scenery here. Having reached Vilnius, even the great cultural trends seemed to subside, and to take on a smaller scale when faced with the creativity of its nature.

The earliest known written sources attesting to the existence of Vilnius are the letters of Grand Duke Gediminas, sent to Western Europe in 1323. Even then Vilnius was probably a fair sized city, for Gediminas was promising his protection to the monks, arti-

100
View of the city from the Aušros Vartai side
101
Aušros Vartai chapel. 18th–19th C.

sans, and merchants whom he invited to settle there. But though legends attribute the glory of the founding of the city to Gediminas, he was in fact not responsible for its coming into being. For economic and strategic reasons, during the Middle Ages rulers usually had more than one capital city, and Lithuania was apparently no exception. Vilnius was such a centre along with Trakai and Kernavė in the time of Grand Duke Mindaugas (d. 1263), and excavations of the Vilnius castles have confirmed that the city had already been a capital under his rule.

Vilnius grew rapidly during the early Middle Ages, for it found itself not only at the crossroads of trading routes, but also of Eastern and Western civilizations. Living where cultures and religions intersected, Vilnius residents learned to have a tolerant attitude towards that which differed. Catholic and Orthodox churches were being built in a pagan environment, and even when Catholicism became the state religion, quite a number of

high state officials were of the Orthodox faith. Vilnius (Vilna) was a centre of Jewish culture, known as Jerusalem of the North. Living conditions here formulated a distinctive ethnic type – the so-called Litvaks, who were known amongst other Jews for their education, rational thinking, and dignified bearing. Vilnius became a centre of Jewish faith and Talmudic studies, a venue for fierce debates between Hassidim and Orthodox, and the home of the Gaon of Vilna (rabbi Elijah ben Judah Solomon Zalman, 1720–1797), a world famous philosopher and an ideologist who rejected the heresy of Hassidism. In later times, Vilnius was also known as the capital of Yiddish: during the inter-war period, the Strashun Library had the largest collection of books in this language.

Ethnic communities usually settled in one place, and those places can be traced according to still existing street-names – Žydų ("Jewish"), Vokiečių ("German"), Rusų ("Russian"), Totorių ("Tartar")...

By the beginning of the 16th C., Vilnius was a real city: approximately one hundred 2–3 storey high stone buildings sat within the defence walls, church towers spiralled upward, a Renaissance Lower Castle sat at the foot of Pilies Hill, and the River Neris boasted its first bridge (a good while later it was painted and thereby acquired the name "Green Bridge"). With the spread of Renaissance and humanistic ideas, the city became the cultural centre of Eastern Europe. The Renaissance concept of the joy and splendour of life had much in common with the philosophy of Grand Duke Sigismund Augustus. Following the example of the rulers of other countries, he transformed the Vilnius castles into a truly royal estate: he invited masters from Italy, and built himself a beautiful palace. Even the Papal Nuncio was impressed, claiming that the treasure he had seen in Venice, and those owned by the Pope could not compare with what Vilnius had – an abundance of wealth, ornamented dishes, splendid man-size clocks, musical instruments, etc. When Sigismund Augustus resided in Vilnius, nearly 1,000 people directed his entertainment and ceremonial affairs. But the royal estate was not only known for its celebrations, banquets and tournaments – it was also a centre for culture, a venue for scholarly debates, literary evenings, choral performances, visits by travelling actors and

102
*Great Courtyard at the Vilnius University
and the Church of St. John with belfry*

103
*Terrestrial globe, dedicated to Grand Duke of Lithuania Augustus III.
White Hall at the Vilnius University*

104
Main University building

105
*View of the Presidency and University towers
from the Presidential garden*

106
Šv. Jono St.

107
Pilies St.

musicians. It had a massive art collection. Second according to size in Europe, the royal estate library contained over 4,000 books – more than the royal library in Cracow. The Grand Duke had typically Renaissance library, with the most celebrated 16th C. publications of the classics, law and the natural sciences, medicine, military literature, travelogues, etc. (After the death of Sigismund Augustus, this treasure was inherited by the Vilnius University.)

One of the developments conforming to Renaissance laws was the appearance of the printed word. The honour of being the first printer in Vilnius (and in the whole of the Grand Duchy of Lithuania) goes to the founder of the written word in Belarus, Skoryna: he printed *Apostle* and *Small Book of Travels* in Vilnius in 1525. Publishing grew rapidly with an increasing polemic between the Reformationists and the Catholics. During the Reformation period every religious community sought to have its own printing house, and books were printed in Russian, Polish, Latin, Latvian, and Lithuanian. Religious literature for all European Jews was published in Vilnius. The University Printers, which issued the first Lithuanian books in the GDL, and printed

books in the Slavic, Latin, Lithuanian, and Latin languages, functioned for 200 years. (Book shops appeared in Vilnius either somewhat before, or during the mid-17th C.)

In 1569, the Jesuits were invited to Vilnius to oppose the Reformation movement. In 1570 they founded a college, and in 1579 one of the first schools of higher learning in Eastern Europe (the first in Vilnius) – the *Almae academia et universitas Vilnensis societatis Jesu*. With all of its ethnic groups, languages, and religions, with its marvellous harmony of diverse architectural styles and nature, with its Renaissance-fostered luminaries, Vilnius offered the perfect terrain for starting and developing a university. Instruction was in Latin, and students arrived from nearly the whole of Europe (including Spain). Although initially out of touch with the most important cultural centres of the period, Vilnius University fairly soon became one of the most distinctive harbingers of science and culture in Europe. A collection of poems by Sarbievius, a graduate and professor at the University, entitled *Lyricorum libri tres* (title page designed by Rubens), was published dozens of times in various languages throughout Europe. *Logic* by Prof. Martynas Smigleckis became popular in schools in England and France (Johnathan Swift solved questions from it

during exams at the Dublin University). In 1650, Vilnius University graduate Kazimieras Semenavičius published a treatise in Amsterdam entitled *Ars magna artilleriae*, which was translated into French, English, and German, and used for 150 years as the most authoritative text on artillery in Europe. Here for the first time were theories on rocket technology and attempts to find practical applications for multi-stage rockets and for the concept of rocket based artillery. In 1753, Tomas Žebrauskas and benefactress Elzbieta Oginskaitė-Puzinienė established an astronomical observatory at the University – the oldest in Eastern Europe, and the fourth oldest in the world. The list of works by Vilnius University graduates and professors could go on (many of their names have been inscribed in gold lettering on the walls of the arcade in the Great Courtyard), but perhaps it suffices to say that although established at an earlier date, the nearest universities in Cracow and Königsberg did not make as great an impact as did Vilnius University.

Despite the changing times, governments and ideologies, the Vilnius University maintained its high status. During the 19th C. it was being lauded by great Polish romantics – Adam Mickiewicz, Juliusz Słowacki, Józef Kraszewski, Antoni Odyniec – who called themselves Lithuanians, and who declared their love for this country. A geologist by the name of Ignas Domeika reached Chile after the uprising of 1831 in Lithuania; he was elected rector of the University of Santiago, and using Lithuania's example, developed a system of education for that country. A ridge of mountains, the city of Domeyko, a type of plant, and a mineral

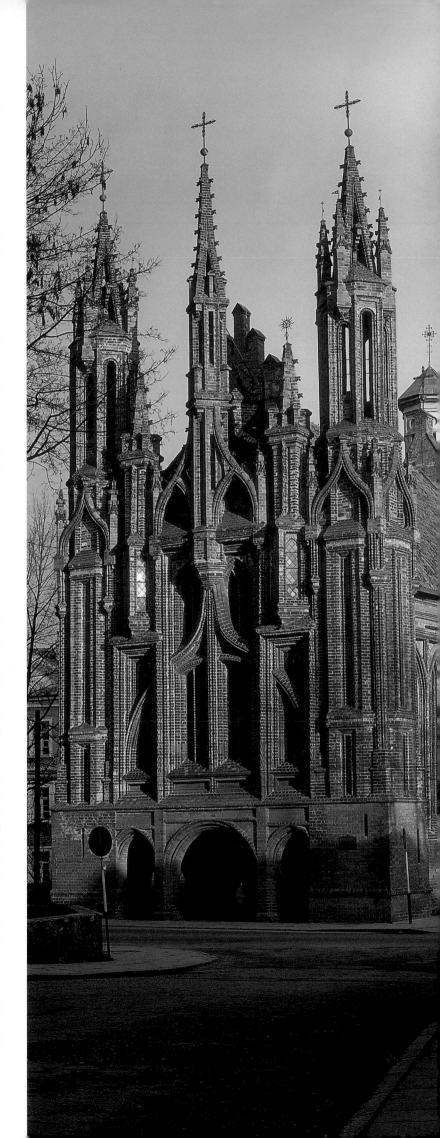

108
Church of the Bernardines
109
Church of St. Anne. 1501

that he discovered were all named after this man in honour of his contributions to Chile.

In the second half of the 20th C., the Vilnius University was known for its Lithuanian School of Mathematics, which analysed the theory of probabilities created by its long-time rector Jonas Kubilius; awards have gone to University experts in cardiac surgery, under the leadership of Algimantas Marcinkevičius; and the Centre of Baltic Philology is famous for its extensive and unique scholarly works in the sphere of comparative linguistics.

During the 17th–18th C., Vilnius acquired a Baroque form. It is mostly the architecture from that period that has survived to this day. Though Gothic in lay-out – with small winding streets and triangle-shaped squares throughout the Old Town – Vilnius is called a Baroque city. The towers and pediments of the Churches of the Missionaries, St. Theresa, All Saints, and St. Casimir present stately panoramic accents; their billowing silhouettes echo and extend the lines of the cityscape.

At the end of the 18th C., classicism gave the city its stricter architectural features. The most important buildings – the Cathedral, Town Hall, and mansions of the nobility – were built or renovated in this style. But it was political, not cultural developments which were the most decisive for Vilnius in the 19th C. When Lithuania became a province of Russia – and thereby a northwestern territory – signs of its former sovereignty began to be effaced. Part of the city wall and gates, and the Lower Castle were torn down, Catholic churches were turned into Orthodox

ones, monasteries into army barracks. The University was closed. As Vilnius was the third largest city in the Russian Empire (after Petersburg and Moscow), the idea was to rejuvenate it according to a plan applied to many of its cities (including Kaunas) at that time. The principal street of the new city centre – the present Gedimino Prospect – began to be laid in 1836; it stretched from the Old Town to an Orthodox church in the suburb of Žvėrynas.

Vilnius underwent few changes during the early 1900s, when it travelled from one set of hands to another. However, by the end of the Second World War, after the Holocaust, repatriations, and bombings, it looked like a wilderness.

The worst period for what had been a rich architectural legacy occurred in the few decades following the war. "Modernization"

110
Church of the Bonifratres. 17th–18th C.
111
Dominikonų St. with the Church of St. John belfry in the distance
112
Interior of the Church of St. Peter and St. Paul

of the Old Town, and construction of new typical suburbs was undertaken following a general plan created for Vilnius in 1953 according to a Soviet concept of urbanization. Fortunately, a fairly large portion of one of the largest (256 ha) and most valuable Old Towns in Eastern Europe survived. The Vilnius Old Town has been added to the list of UNESCO world cultural heritage sites. The last years have seen a period of rapid restoration of buildings and old street pavements; the Old Town is truly becoming a prestigious area for institutions and homes. Vilnius is changing from the capital of a former Soviet republic to the centre of a European state – with a preserved and publicly posted history, an intensive cultural and political life, and an increasingly strengthening economy.

113
Cathedral and belfry

114
*Statue of Grand Duke Alexander
in the Cathedral Chapel of St. Casimir*

Kaunas

It appears that Kaunas, the provisional capital of Lithuania during the inter-war period, will hold on to its status for some years to come.

Like many of the early towns, Kaunas was founded along a waterway, at the confluence of the Nemunas and Neris rivers. A stone castle, one of the most important fortifications in Lithuania's battles against the Crusaders, was built here in the 13th C. The city expanded around the castle, especially after the victorious Battle of Grunwald in 1410. Also established and still surviving from the beginning of that century were churches, monasteries, and a school. Kaunas grew rapidly because of its convenient location (with a port on the River Nemunas at one time); by the 16th C. it was a city of wealthy merchants and artisans. Several centuries later, however, its importance as a commercial centre diminished and its development came to a halt.

The city changed drastically when it became the most important western border citadel of czarist Russia. Its centre moved from the old town to the new town, and the city laid its principal street – the present Laisvės Ave. Kaunas was encircled by forts and other military constructions, making it a first class Russian stronghold. On the eve of the First World War, military fortifications covered an area measuring 65 square km and the garrison included 90,000 people (with a population of approx. 100,000). Nevertheless, this glorious fortress was conquered fairly easily by the advancing German army. At the end of the 19th C., the city had also become a centre for the national movement and for the dissemination of a prohibited Lithuanian press.

The inter-war period was an exceptional one in the history of the city's development. When Lithuania lost Vilnius to the Poles, Kaunas became the provisional capital – with all the accompanying government institutions, schools of higher learning (including the Vytautas Magnus University), theatres, publishing houses, museums (the War Museum, M.K. Čiurlionis Art

115
Town Square with the confluence of the Nemunas and Neris rivers in the distance
116
Town Square. Cathedral-Basilica. 15th–17th C.

Gallery), and newspapers. A grimy toy fortress became a capital of Europe. The majority of new buildings – the Bank of Lithuania, Parliament and Justice buildings (now the Philharmonic), and the M.K. Čiurlionis Gallery – were built in a neo-classical style; the city theatre was reconstructed in a modernized baroque style. The flourishing of a functional aesthetic in the 1930s prompted Kaunas architects to incorporate overtones of functionalism, constructivism and stylistic expressionism in their designs. The city acquired new institutions, cinemas, schools, and residential buildings in a variety of architectural styles.

Although during the Soviet period Kaunas lost its official status as the capital of Lithuania, it did remain the spiritual centre of the nation. Even after the deportations and repressions, Kaunas

retained a fair number of its old city-dwellers, survivors from the independence period. The people of Kaunas were always the most persistent resistance fighters. The death of Romas Kalanta, his self-immolation by fire in protest against the occupation, and resulting student disturbances in the spring of 1972 widely publicized the city whose principal street even in the Soviet period held on to the name Laisvės ("Freedom") Ave. The Lithuanian men's basketball team had won the European championship title several times during the inter-war period – a significant achievement, adding a great deal to creating a new picture of Lithuania. In the Soviet times, the defeat of the Moscow team by the Kaunas "Žalgiris" basketball players matched Lithuania's greatest diplomatic victories of the early 1900s: these were moments representing the nation's solidarity, pride and triumph, and ultimately – a legal form of resistance. Even today, the city is best known for basketball, with player Arvydas Sabonis in the role of the world's most famous Kaunas resident.

117
Pažaislis church and convent on the banks of the Kaunas Bay. 17th–18th C.

118
Museum of Literature (building – 17th C.) and a monument to poet Maironis (sculptor Gediminas Jokūbonis, 1977)

119
North side of the Town Square

Klaipėda

Lithuania's seaport established itself on both sides of the mouth of the River Danė near the strait which connects the Curonian Lagoon to the Baltic Sea. Its origins date from the mid-13th C., when it was a castle built by the Teutonic Order. The castle was called Memelburg, the city developing around it – Memel. Its Courish name – Klaipėda – is mentioned in written sources in 1423. The city's founding and its later history are linked to Prussia and to Germany. The Old Town of Klaipėda is unlike any other in Lithuania: the houses are of a strict format with a fair amount of fachwerk (timber work), the streets laid out in regular blocks. One doesn't need to be an expert to feel the Prussian

influence. The German language and a Protestant spirit dominated here for many years. Warehouses, a waterside, boat masts and winches give the city a distinctive harbour atmosphere.

The years 1807–08 are historically significant for the present German nation: at that time, Prussian King Friedrich Wilhelm II (who had been beaten by Napoleon), and his wife sought refuge in Klaipėda – which briefly became the capital of Prussia. A decree abolishing serfdom in Prussia was proclaimed here in 1807.

Klaipėda began to expand again in the 19th C. with the manufacture of fertilizers and machinery, and the introduction of ship building. The Wilhelm Canal was excavated to connect the River Minija to the Curonian Lagoon. The city acquired a post office building and a magistracy; its new town began to expand. At the turn of the century, it was a true working-class city: approximately 2,500 people were employed in its 70 or so enterprises.

120
Klaipėda harbour
121
Gateway to the harbour

Books began to be printed in the Lithuanian language in Klaipėda in 1825, and it became an important centre for Lithuanian publication in the time of the press ban: the usual gothic script continued to be used for books for the inhabitants of Lithuania Minor, while those for the Lithuanians under czarist rule were printed in a latin script.

In 1923, the territory of Klaipėda was joined to Lithuania, though the rhythm of daily life hardly changed until the end of the Second World War – which devastated the centre, and damaged the Old Town and the city's churches. The evacuation of 1945 also cleared Klaipėda of its old inhabitants. After the war, it was taken over by people who had no interest in the city's tradi-

122
Old Post Office. End of 19th C.
123
Aukštoji St.
124
Monument to poet Simon Dach – "Annchen von Tharau"
(reconstructed in 1990)

tions or history – i.e., by harried labourers, homeless peasants, nomads from the expanses of Russia. The churches and cemeteries were completely razed to the ground, as were monuments reflecting its Germanic history. Klaipėda became a city of factories, and a harbour with blocks of typical apartment buildings. It was not until the 1970s that the atmosphere began to change: during that period Klaipėda acquired branches of the music conservatory, a faculty of the Šiauliai Pedagogical Institute, a Watch Museum and a Maritime Museum, a sculpture park, and renovation works in the Old Town.

The restoration of Independence brought with it a university, new churches, the reconstruction of certain monuments. The harbour was modernized and used more intensively, for it is the only ice-free port on the eastern shores of the Baltic. Careful restoration of its past is building a new Klaipėda.

Šiauliai

Šiauliai is the principal city in northern Lithuania, close to the main road between Vilnius and Riga. The history of the city's origins is marked by the Battle of Saulė in 1236, when a joint army of Lithuanian, Samogitian, and Latvian dukes totally vanquished the attacking Teutonic Order.

Vilnius St. is the principal city axis. Most of the city's industrial enterprises were located here in the 19th C., and before the First World War it boasted 2 film theatres. Now it is taken up by shops, restaurants, and cafes – with finely executed exteriors from the 1970s–80s.

The Renaissance Church of St. Peter and St. Paul (1617–34), a unique fortress-like construction, is the oldest building in Šiauliai. Its 70.7 m high tower is visible from all directions, and one needs only to follow it in order to reach the centre of the city.

Another city landmark is "Sukilėlių kalnelis" ("Rebel Hill"), a monument to the uprising of 1863, which involved many people from around the area: 600 rebels fought near Šiauliai on April 15. The czarist government suppressed the uprising and enacted repressive measures, executing 11 rebels on this site.

An old city, Šiauliai was constantly ravaged by fires, devastated by Swedish and French armies, and seriously damaged during the First and Second World Wars; the only surviving remnants of the Old Town include a tidy classic network of streets from the latter half of the 18th C., with a square in the centre near the church. The

125
Hill of Crosses
126
Church of St. Peter and St. Paul. 17th C.

city had been restructured at the initiative of Grand Duchy of Lithuania treasurer Antanas Tyzenhauzas, economic administrator of Šiauliai. He began to create an industrial centre with several factories, including for the manufacture of textiles (producing magnificent linen and fine wool cloth), and beer (the famous "Gubernija" brewery – the city's oldest functioning industry). A confectionery factory was established in 1876; its delicious candies continue to promote the name of the city. The industrial sector flourished here when the city was intersected by the Petersburg-Königsberg highway in 1858, and by the Romny-Liepaja railway in 1871.

A much later, but equally important date in the city's industrial history is 1951, when the bicycle factory made its first "Ereliukas" bicycles. Šiauliai became widely known for these and "Kregždutė" bikes for teenagers, and later for its "Venta" and "Rambynas" folding bicycles. Bicycles changed the city's image and way of life. Šiauliai became a bicycle city, and actively encouraged this environmentally safe form of transportation: a bicycle path was built in 1981, the streets are equipped with bicycle lanes and a square for children's bikes, and bicycle competitions are held here.

Palanga

Not every famous world resort has the clean and soft sand that one finds at Palanga, the largest seaside resort in Lithuania – with beaches which stretch for approximately 20 km. Palanga is also known for its unique souvenirs: in stormy weather, the waves throw long braids of seaweed up onto the shores – in them, with luck, one can find tiny pieces of amber.

On arrival in Palanga, holidaymakers first rush down to the sea. But the town itself also has interesting sights. A botanical park, whose western border reaches the beach, was first established at the end of the 19th C. Approximately 200 (formerly 500) types of trees and bushes grown from imported plants (mostly from botanical gardens in Paris and Berlin), can be found among the native pines. In the centre of the park is the rich Amber Museum (with 5,000 items on exhibit; 30,000 items in the depository), which was opened in 1963. The Museum is housed in the former residence (built at the beginning of the 20th C.) of Count Felix Tyszkiewicz. Count Tyszkiewicz is in fact the true founder of

127
Amber Museum
128
Villas along Birutės St.
129
Palanga pier

the resort. Along with the residential manor, he built the White Villa, "Kurhauz", and other summer houses, tended to the park, and brought in electricity.

On Birutės Hill, which also stands in the park, is a small octagonal red brick chapel; at the foot of the hill – a grotto and an altar. According to legend, this was a pagan sanctuary, where priestess Birutė, later the wife of Grand Duke Kęstutis, kindled the sacred fire.

Back in the 12th–13th C., Palanga was a trade centre, and in the 16th C. – a popular port, competing successfully with both Riga and Klaipėda. In 1701, at the bidding of Riga merchants, the Swedish army tore down the Palanga harbour and buried it in rocks. In the latter half of the 19th C. the Counts Tyszkiewicz, who owned the city, decided to restore the harbour. They built an oak bridge, at which boats would anchor, and a dyke with rails (along present-day Basanavičiaus St.) leading to the pier. Bricks were hauled from this pier to Liepaja on the steamer "Phoenix" several times a week. When shifting sands covered the western part of

Palanga and the pier, the bridge became a favourite walking place for vacationers. Palanga's career as a port finally ended, and the town eventually became a resort.

Palanga has been known as a holiday spot since the beginning of the 19th century. In July and August, people would come even from abroad to swim in the sea basins. Adam Mickiewicz vacationed in Palanga in 1824, and immortalized the site in his lines.

In 1937, Palanga had 36 private villas and 5 sanatoriums. A pharmacy which opened in 1827 still operates there; it manufactured a tincture according to an old Lithuanian recipe which used 27 medicinal herbs – it was called "Trejos devynerios" ("Three times nine"). Drops for the heart were also made here (according to a recipe by Klaipėda doctor Schroeder), and exported abroad.

Sea, sun, fresh air, pine forests, mineral waters, mud baths and a variety of entertainment – one can find it all at Lithuania's most popular resort.

130
The sea at sunset
131
Amber treasures from Juodkrantė
132
Amber piece with inclusion

The publisher is grateful to the following museums for their permission to use illlustrations:

Lithuanian National Museum
Lithuanian Art Museum
National M.K. Čiurlionis Art Museum
Klaipėda Regional Museum
"Aušra" Museum in Šiauliai
"Alka" Museum in Telšiai
Amber Gallery in Nida

Contents

Cover: Zapyškis church. 16th C.
Title page: View from Šatrija, the highest hill in Žemaitija
Introductory page: Trakai Island Castle,
residence of Lithuania's rulers in the 15th C.

Text by Audra Kairienė

Design by Isaak Zibuts

Photographs by Arūnas Baltėnas, Eugenijus Drobelis, Vytautas Knyva,
Raimondas Paknys, Juozas Polis, Henrikas Sakalauskas, Kęstutis Stoškus

Translated from Lithuanian by Vida Urbonavičius-Watkins

© R. Paknio leidykla, 2002
R. Paknys Publishing House, Išganytojo 4-10, 2001 Vilnius
Tel. +370 5 2629950, fax +370 5 2123156
centras@paknioleidykla.lt
ISBN 9986-830-49-4